MW01123170

Under Siege
The Federal NDP in the Nineties

Ian McLeod

James Lorimer & Company, Publishers
Toronto, 1994

James Lorimer & Company Ltd. acknowledges with thanks the support of the Canada Council, the Ontario Arts Council and the Ontario Publishing Centre in the development of writing and publishing in Canada.

Canadian Cataloguing in Publication Data
  McLeod, Ian, 1953-
  Under siege: The federal NDP in the nineties

Includes bibliographical references and index.
ISBN 1-55028-455-X (bound) ISBN 1-55028-454-1 (pbk.)

1. New Democratic Party. 2. Canada. Parliament - Elections, 1993.
3. Canada - Politics and government - 1993 - .
I. Title.

JL197.N4M35 1994   324.27107   C94-931909-0

James Lorimer & Company Ltd., Publishers
35 Britain Street
Toronto, Ontario M5A 1R7

Printed and bound in Canada

Contents

	Introduction	v
1	Wanted: A New Party	1
2	The Leadership	17
3	In Search of Ms. McLaughlin	33
4	A Caucus Adrift	49
5	Adieu, Québec	66
6	Dreams and Economics	85
7	The 1993 Campaign	100
8	A Better Umbrella	116
9	The Virtue of Patience	131
	Notes	147
	Bibliography	156
	Index	157

Table 1

Federal NDP Election Results 1962-1993

Year	Seats	Percentage of Total Vote
1962	19	13.50
1963	17	13.10
1965	21	17.90
1968	22	17.00
1972	31	17.70
1974	16	15.40
1979	26	17.70
1980	32	19.80
1984	30	18.70
1988	43	20.40
1993	9	7.40

Source: Adapted from Alan Whitehorn, *Canadian Socialism* (Toronto: Oxford University Press, 1991)

Introduction

The New Democratic Party of Canada faces an uncertain future after its disastrous election loss of October 1993. At the same time, the Canadian left outside electoral politics shows continued vitality through the work of trade unions and thousands of social action groups. At least for now, it appears many voters no longer see the party as a political voice for social change.

A post-election opinion survey reported that only 26 per cent of those who voted NDP in 1988 returned to the party in 1993, while 27 per cent went to the Liberals. In this sample, the NDP also lost 14 per cent of its strength to the Reform Party and 6 per cent to the Bloc Québécois. Fourteen per cent of former NDP voters simply stayed home.[1]

This book explores some of the reasons behind the NDP's collapse and poses some questions about what comes next. It is based partly on a journal I began in summer 1992 when I worked as a writer for the NDP on Parliament Hill. After a season of popularity and a few dreams of glory, the party had nose-dived in the polls. Our in-house survey that August put us at 10 per cent overall — far behind the Liberals, and even behind Mulroney's Conservatives. The NDP "universe" — the tally of all those who might consider voting for us — had shrivelled to 30 per cent, down from more than 50 per cent in early 1991.

The outlook grew bleaker as the months passed. Strategists and caucus assistants watched for a rebound. One said repeatedly: "The federal campaign used to be a marathon, but now it's a sprint. This campaign's going to be a sprint, and we have to get ready for it." Then, one by one, we abandoned our hopes for government, for Official Opposition status, for a decent showing. We passed through denial, anger, resignation, acceptance. By June 1993, when I was working at the federal headquarters, we expected the worst. In the words of federal secretary Fraser Green, we rode out the fall campaign in the surreal calm that goes with "a really good car crash."[2]

On October 25, 1993, Canada's New Democrats took nine seats, all in the West, with 7 per cent of the vote. This was a smaller vote share than the CCF got in the 1958 election that sealed its doom. In Ontario, with an NDP majority government in power, the party finished in fourth place or worse in 70 of 99 ridings. Eighteen NDP candidates in Quebec collected fewer votes than the yogic flyers of the Natural Law Party. New Democrats spoke on election night of "moving forward" and "putting this setback behind us." By March of 1994, the federal party's support in the polls had slid further, to 4 per cent.

Some loyalists insist the NDP had no control over events between 1989 and 1993. They blame its collapse on outside forces: the public's fierce desire to crush the Mulroney Conservatives, unpopular NDP provincial governments, cynical news media, a worldwide loss of confidence in social democratic policies. The Conservatives' surrender of Canadian sovereignty and the loss of hundreds of thousands of good jobs had created paranoia, fed intolerance and divided the left.

All these points carry some weight, but they do not let the NDP off the hook. The party faces extinction. The leadership and active members are now formally committed to a review of the NDP's structure and policies. When the time comes to act, they can decide to preserve in every detail the institution that David Lewis built before 1961, or they can choose fundamental change. Neither course will guarantee survival.

One of the saddest aspects of the current dilemma is that the NDP sensed the need for change several years ago, and nothing happened. Like other candidates in the 1989 leadership race, Audrey McLaughlin responded to a restless mood in the party by promising to change the way decisions were made. She talked about "a team approach," and "revitalizing the party" by "working with communities and regions."

"The fact is that, as a woman, I can bring a fresh perspective to many of the issues facing us today."[3]

McLaughlin restated these themes in her 1992 book, *A Woman's Place*. She argued that she and other women were prepared to create a new kind of politics in Canada. She said the party should widen consultation, broaden its membership, and work more effectively with social action groups.

However, the federal NDP is rooted in old habits. McLaughlin brought passion and intelligence to her job, a lack of experience, and whatever liabilities ride with a woman leader in a male-run party and parliament. Her good intentions brought limited results.

In a period when the NDP had its largest-ever caucus in Parliament, it lost public support. It left women, young people, aboriginal people and new Canadians unmoved. The party had made its reputation defending social programs, but when NDP governments came to power in the provinces they found themselves cutting deficits and restraining spending. The federal party has still not come to terms with how these provincial actions have changed its future.

During the Charlottetown negotiations when Canadians focused their attention on events in Ottawa, the NDP joined the Liberals and Conservatives on the constitutional Yes committee. At best, this established the NDP as a junior partner alongside the older parties. Hundreds of party members wrote and telephoned to condemn the Yes committee, calling it an élite attempt to hijack the people's right to decide.

As the general election approached, the federal Liberals picked up the popular slogans in the New Democrat platform. They promised to protect medicare and create jobs. For the first time in a generation, centrist and left-liberal voters in the West flocked to the Liberals. So did a majority of voters in Ontario.

Former NDP supporters went to the Liberals because they didn't see the NDP as radical or effective, and because the NDP had lost track of where it stood on many economic questions.[4] They went to Reform because they didn't see the NDP as a check on the traditional parties or as a bulwark against the demands of Quebec. They went to the Bloc because the NDP presented no coherent program in favour of Quebec.

At a time of widespread economic hardship, the New Democratic Party failed to prove the need for a social democratic voice in federal politics. In the last days of the campaign, the party simplified its message to a single point: that Canada needs New Democrats in Parliament. The party's nightly polls, carried out in its most promising ridings, suggested that only one in four voters agreed.

The NDP has lost three-quarters of its MPs and 80 per cent of its parliamentary staff. It has lost the right to ask daily questions in the Commons, and to serve on Commons committees. The federal headquarters employs half a dozen workers. In early 1994, the party council agreed on a process for renewal; in April, with the party on the verge of financial ruin, a panic-driven executive cancelled the summer convention that was to have launched the process; when angry members protested, the executive agreed to organize an informal summer policy conference. During the same period, McLaughlin submitted her resignation at least twice; but with no obvious successor in sight, and no consensus on how to choose a successor, the executive persuaded McLaughlin to stay on.

At the grass roots, many who supported the NDP in the past have departed, grieving for an institution they believe no longer represents them. Some who remain fear any change, and believe the party will recover only if it sticks to its traditional message. They will be supported by those provincial party workers in the West who view open discussion at the federal level as a threat to the NDP's chances in the provinces.

I have great respect for the people I worked with in seven years inside the New Democratic Party. I have not written this book in a mood of spite or mischief. I have tried to indicate a few lines for debate, not as a previously overlooked Moses but as a journeyman political worker with access to diverse sources. I believe the NDP must undergo a thorough renewal, in consultation with labour, the social action movements, former New Democrats and non-New Democrats. I hope this account may help in that renewal. Without some new spirit of commitment and reorganization in the federal NDP, it will campaign in the next election only as an offshoot of a few provincial parties, and will ultimately fade away.

This would be a loss for Canada. As Allan Blakeney puts it, the people who run the market economy will not be deflected from their course by delegations or briefs, but only by power.[5] There are many and increasing centres of power outside of parliaments and legislatures; all the same, the threat of social democratic power at the ballot box, and the actions of NDP governments in the provinces, have kept all Canadian governments on their toes for decades and have made this a better country.

I would like to thank James Lorimer, the Douglas-Coldwell Foundation and the Ontario Arts Council for supporting this project. I also want to thank those who reviewed draft chapters: Chris Hunter, Tom McLeod, Terry O'Grady, John Young, Leslie Kerr, Gerald Caplan, Angus Ricker, Raymond Guardia, Caroline Andrew, Eileen Dooley, Bruce Tate, Brian Topp, Danl Loewen, Ish Theilheimer, Stephen Learey, Bill Knight, Alan Whitehorn and Elisabeth Arnold; also Mary Ann Carmichael and Marnee Manson for research assistance, and Andrew Nau for technical assistance.

A special thanks goes to everyone who agreed to share their views. In a few cases I have withheld their names, although I have tried to keep this practice to a minimum.

1

Wanted: A New Party

What is Canada? Some might say it's just a motley crowd on the make. What does Canada stand for, anyway? Ah, yes, it's a great country to make money in — especially if you have money to begin with. Where will Canada be in the distant future — say, toward the end of this century? Perhaps we'll be headed along the same road as the United States, a nation owned by multi-millionaires ... We need a new political party, before our resources are seized! We need a party that will have what no present party commands: moral enthusiasm!

— Dr. Salem Bland, from an address to a Sunday
People's Forum, Winnipeg, 1913[1]

SPRING 1994, and the New Democratic Party is searching for It again. Fighting off financial ruin and split over basic questions of strategy, the NDP must also redefine its vision and try to convince large numbers of Canadians that the vision makes sense in the real world. The Bloc works in Ottawa for Quebec sovereignty, the Reform Party for an end to activist government; the NDP drifts.

"Will this book tell us what It is?" asks the federal secretary, his brow furrowed. "The executive's not asking for much — they just want me to come up with It." As the federal secretary knows, the problem goes with the territory. Over time, the NDP has enjoyed just enough provincial success to keep it alive. At the federal level, the party goes from analysing the last loss to preparing for the next one.[2]

Newspaper editorials say it's time for the NDP to "rekindle its inner fire." On this issue, party supporters agree with the editorial writers. How can an organization "steeped in protest and rebellion"[3] lose ground at a time when angry voters are looking for change? Have the leaders lost sight of the goal? Have the strategists forgotten the party's roots?

Life used to be simpler for activists on the left, back in the days before anyone paid them much attention. They knew where they wanted to take Canada, and they knew how to inspire and motivate. James Woodsworth had only to walk on the hillside above Montreal to hear music and see the future before him.

> In this city of homes, I thought I could discern the indistinct outlines of the workplaces of the future. To these, men and women went forth not as dumb, driven cattle, but eagerly, as the artist to his studio, or as a child to his play. They worked together not as slaves, not as jealous rivals, but as partners in a common enterprise.[4]

Surrounded by the promise of a new country, the early radicals could enjoy a euphoric mood. Speakers and audiences believed that society was evolving towards perfection. They shared their "moral enthusiasm" for hours at a stretch in labour halls and village schoolhouses.

After 30 years of agitation, they formed a party — the CCF — that prescribed state action as the cure for Canada's ills. Government would run key businesses, set prices, control incomes, and "replace the present capitalist system." The founding manifesto promised "a proper collective organization of our economic resources such as will make possible a greater degree of leisure and a much richer individual life for every citizen."[5]

The crusading language and zeal of the early CCF remain a legend — and a burden — within the modern NDP. The legend overlooks the CCF's general unpopularity with Canadian voters, and it ignores the pragmatic shift that started in the 1940s, a shift that transformed the CCF into the moderate-left New Democratic Party in 1961. Perhaps New Democrats have forgotten their past, in forgetting their party's long evolution towards compromise; they also live uneasily in the present, and look pessimistically towards the future.

The political environment has changed since 1933, and since 1961. The optimism of pioneering days is gone. Voters are anxious about their prospects, sceptical of politicians, awash in information and pseudo-information. Rather than lecturing at mass meetings, today's radicals jostle with rival TV panelists between beer commercials. The state, grown large with the blessing of the CCF/NDP, has also become bureaucratic and costly. Many working people view it as a problem, not a solution. Political parties decline in importance. Socially conscious citizens join issue groups instead, because the issues are closer to home, the work more fun, and the victories more tangible.

Social democrats walk a rough road. In the midst of a party crisis, they must prove that their work matters to people, and that social democratic governments make a difference. The acrimony and petty politics inherent in debating a new direction may tear the movement to shreds; and if it survives, there is still no guarantee that the old NDP support will ever come back. On the other hand, if the movement backs away from the challenge of renewal, it is likely to die of old age and apathy.

Various groups in the NDP have started to discuss the party's future. Their work points to an enormous task: a need for a rebuilding process that will make full use of available brainpower and generate (for the first time in many years) a widespread appeal among young people.

The guidelines for such a process emerge clearly from the writings and speeches of Audrey McLaughlin, if not from her actions. To carry any weight, the new consensus must be broadly based and genuine. It cannot be worked out on a flip chart by two or three senior staff, or by an advertising agency over the course of a weekend, or over the phone by provincial barons. Leaders in the NDP and labour must invest time and patience, and accept that some differences will be aired in public and some results will be beyond their control.

Some supporters want to reconstruct the NDP as a permanent party of opposition, to allow the widest possible scope for visions and radical proposals. But most, I believe, agree with Ed Broadbent: "Social democratic politics involves both principles and power. To argue only for principles is to be narcissistically self-indulgent."[6] To be serious and effective, the party must prepare to govern — to take charge of a federal state created by the Liberal and Conservative parties amid corporate pressures. The NDP must look beyond its loyalty to organized groups and their claims and decide how it will manage government in a hard-headed and efficient way.

In 1993, the federal NDP's confusion about its ability to govern crippled its ability to campaign. Public hostility towards the Rae government in Ontario had grown so intense that some federal NDP candidates feared to leave their homes. In the late spring, a federal campaign planner heaved himself down after a long, frustrating and inconclusive wrangle on the phone with Audrey McLaughlin. "Gee, I guess it would be awful if we got wiped out," he said, and paused. "But you know what? It would be a lot worse if we won."

The NDP symbolizes "social democracy under siege" in capitalist North America.[7] New Democrats have influenced Canada in many ways, through provincial governments and through persuasion in opposition, day after day, decade after decade. They have shaped socialized health care, advocated for poorer regions and disadvantaged people, and built support for international development and peace. At the same time, the possibilities for achieving a socialist commonwealth in Canada have grown increasingly remote. In an era of victories for corporate capitalism, New Democrats have fought a long retreat, and acquired a reputation as opponents of progress and prophets of doom.

Beginning in the late 1960s, New Democrats sounded the alarm over foreign control of Canadian industry. Many of their predictions proved accurate: Canadian governments lost their former control over the economy, management and research jobs moved to head offices in other countries, and long-term unemployment rose.

In 1983, at the dawn of the Mulroney era, NDP research director James Laxer wrote that the trend towards loss of control would accelerate. "The Canada that will emerge from the new conservatism will be mean-spirited and class-divided. It will be a nation in name only — in reality, little more than a series of regional groupings tied to a declining America."[8]

The U.S.-Canada trade deal formalized the shift of economic control from Canadian governments to international investors. NDP candidates and organized labour warned in 1988 that Canadian governments would lose the power to build Canadian-owned industry through public investment and tax policies. The deal would push governments to reduce business taxes to compete with U.S. regions, and they would forfeit the revenues needed for social programs.

The NDP's official post-1988 view of the world went something like this:

i. Big business has developed a corporate agenda, and the Liberals and Conservatives are ready to put it into effect;

ii. The corporate agenda will strip government of its powers and leave ordinary people defenseless;

iii. Only the NDP has the courage and honesty to speak out.

The North American Free Trade Agreement sharpened the prospect of a bleak corporate-controlled future. Although the opinion polls put NAFTA well down the list of public concerns in 1993, trade union leaders urged the NDP to make the trade agreement with Mexico a key part of the election campaign. In Mexico they saw the industrial slums, the *maquiladoras*, and wondered if this was the future for Canadian workers too — a global *maquiladora*, a beehive world.

The protection afforded by the post-war welfare state, the great achievement of social democracy, is fast disappearing. Labour analyst Guy Standing, in his portrait of current industrial culture, writes global business now demands absolute "flexibility" from working people: that is, a willingness to accept nineteenth-century conditions.

At the top of the social ladder Standing finds the megabosses, men "living at the margins of sanity," obsessed with making the next billion dollars. They hire the upper managers, who draw their incomes increasingly in non-taxable perks, and the "proficians," capitalism's strategists and consultants. In the middle we find "capitalist workers" who still believe the dream — they have saved enough money to buy a small business, or they hope to do so. Beneath them, other full-time workers are caught in a treadmill of harder work, longer hours, and the risk of layoff; and further down, a growing army of "flexworkers" scrape by on low-paid temporary jobs. All of these scramble to stay out of the lowest pool, the millions of permanently unemployed who have become "detached" from the economy.[9]

In contemplating its future, the NDP is caught between this vision of naked class oppression and a desire to retain its image as a moderate party. The party's socialist wing insists that North American capitalism no longer delivers the goods, and working people are ready for a radical message. Wages have stagnated for two decades. Homelessness, almost unknown in Canada 10 years ago, is now commonplace. Canadian élites are developing fraternal ties with a Mexican regime that massacres peasants in the streets. Some say the evils of capitalism have not been this clearly exposed since the 1930s.

However, the 1993 election results hardly suggest a rebirth of class war in Canada. The mood of the NDP focus groups conducted in several cities before the vote illustrates the point. The participants, all chosen from the left side of the political spectrum, viewed government as remote and ineffective. They doubted that any government can protect jobs or social programs. The real power, they said, lies with investors and corporate managers who live outside their world. They expressed bewilderment, sadness, helplessness. But rather than yearning for radical change, they hoped to preserve what they could in their families and neighbourhoods. It is likely that most of these focus-group participants voted Liberal.

For social democrats, the idea of stepping up the attack on the ruling class poses serious electoral hazards. The federal NDP's increasingly shrill "Us-against-Them" rhetoric already appears to focus attention more on the party's shortcomings then on those in power. In labelling working-class and middle-class people as a homogenous mass of victims, the NDP blurs the distinction between well-off wage and salary earners and the poor, and often ends up defending entrenched privilege. At the same time, the Us-against-Them approach places the NDP at odds with anyone who continues to seek and find success in the current system. There is also the matter of the NDP's record in office: a call for class war would sound bogus coming from a party that is forced to deal as constructively as it can with big business whenever it takes power provincially — whether in Saskatchewan in 1944, or in Ontario, British Columbia and Saskatchewan in the 1990s.

Over the years, the leaders and strategists of the federal NDP have wavered over whether to play up class jealousies or respect the ethic of success, and whether to promise revenge against capitalists or a more efficient capitalism. At the founding of the party in 1961, Tommy Douglas cried joyfully that "the common people can beat Money any day of the week." They can't, and the NDP has never spelled out exactly what would happen if they did. The phrase "There is a choice," an interim slogan for Audrey McLaughlin, suggested that ordinary families, standing resolutely behind a people's government, could confront the stock markets, fix the tax system, create jobs and protect medicare. In denouncing the corporate agenda and demanding taxes on the rich, McLaughlin and her MPs raised an important question, but never answered it: Why allow private corporations to function at all?

Ed Broadbent built two federal election campaigns around opposition to the power of big business, but in his 1989 retirement address he cautioned that any plan to dismantle the market system is unreal. "For most thoughtful people, that debate is now closed. Market economies have been responsible for the production of more goods and services since the Second World War than were produced in all of human history."[10]

The deputy leader of the NDP, Nelson Riis, says the party has trifled with class politics for too long. Riis regained his seat in 1993, but lost his status as an official party House Leader. Sitting in his new, cramped quarters, surrounded by boxes, he expressed the hope that the NDP will forget this set of themes.

This whole notion of seeing Canada in a 19th century model of bosses and workers, with us representing the workers, just didn't make sense in this last election at all. We probably got away with it in the past, but the world had changed significantly even in a couple of years. What we represented just didn't fit with the way the world was evolving. Basically, we became the ultimate conservative party. We didn't want this, this, this, and this. And the things that we were in favour of — like universal child care — were such a leap from what we have now that they made us seem extravagant and unreasonable.[11]

Riis speaks for a sometimes overlooked strain in the NDP — the "liberally minded individuals" who, along with labour and the CCF, were originally supposed to form one of the pillars of the new party. Riis argues that to succeed, the NDP must attract small business people and professionals, people with skills, contacts, money and community profile. He suggests that many of them have a social conscience and a commitment to equality that will allow them to work with people from other backgrounds, including labour. They can help build a bridge to larger businesses and set up the partnerships among business, labour and government that Canada needs for economic growth.

Partnerships with corporations? A dead end for the left, says Tony Clarke, a New Democrat supporter and former chair of the Action Canada Network. Clarke led the fight against NAFTA, and believes in regulating corporations more tightly to save jobs and the environment.

These bastards are getting away with blue murder ... Sure they say they're going to pack up and leave. But they are not the ones who are creating jobs. The same companies who said the FTA was going to create jobs have lost or gotten rid of 139,000 jobs over a four-year period ... What's eroding democracy is not what the Reform is talking about. Where it's at is what those corporations are doing to erode our power to exercise any kind of democracy.[12]

The task for the Canadian left in the 1990s is to develop a plan for a productive economy. But the NDP and its allies are split on which road to take, whether to choose confrontation or partnership with capital. This split has the potential to fracture the left into two parties.

Two powerful NDP-affiliated factions, led by the Steelworkers on one side and the Auto Workers on the other, are pulling in opposite directions. The Steelworkers have set out on a course of co-owner-ship and workplace consultation aimed at giving workers a voice in training, management and the investment of profits. The Auto Work-ers have protested that this approach will pave the way for massive concessions. They favour a political strategy of militant unionism and support tough government regulation and taxation. Not coinci-dentally, the Auto Workers have lost patience with the Ontario NDP government, and have diverted money away from the NDP into the social action coalitions.

These two alternatives — partnership and confrontation — imply two competing visions. The Steelworkers want to change the culture of business, increase worker and community ownership of industry, cement the personal ties between managers and workers, and build Canadian firms with a loyalty to the community. This approach suggests both a new confidence and a new pragmatism, a determi-nation that social democracy will play a part, if only a limited part, in shaping North American capitalism. The Auto Workers would return to the grass roots and hope to build a culture of resistance and democratic control. Their approach would reinforce the traditional CCF/NDP division of the world into Us and Them, the common people versus money, "ordinary Canadians" versus unfeeling corpo-rations, a world where the institutions of the left are islands of virtue in a sea of greed.

This disagreement goes to the heart of whether social democracy can survive in a hostile North America. The federal New Democratic Party has long avoided making a choice, resigned to a market econ-omy and yet harshly negative in its attacks on the market's players. Gerry Scott, a veteran party strategist, says that while parties of the democratic left in most countries are actively searching for new approaches in a changing world, the NDP has played at "business as usual."

We have to go back to some basic analysis before we choose a strategy, and from that, tactics will flow. What we've been doing is agreeing on tactics first, and they sometimes get cobbled together into a half-assed and poorly executed strategy. It's been day-to-day tactics driven by the 30-second clip and the desire to be loved by all, and it doesn't work. We have to have fundamental analysis. If that analysis leads us toward more accommodation with capital, so be it. I think it would fail, but that's another question. But let's look at the world in the 1990s, and what it'll be in the next century — what we see is more power for global capital, less power for people, less power for governments, less power for local business.[13]

There is a need for a new consensus and a plan for political action on the Canadian left. Does the NDP have the will or the people to find the answers? Some say the party is closed to new ideas; some reject the party's claims to be democratic. They see an organization run by a clique of political professionals who spend their days talking to themselves.

The make-up of the 1993 central campaign working group might confirm this view. It brought together four senior trade union officials (including the committee chair), four members of the federal leader's staff, one member of Manitoba caucus staff, one member of Parliament, and a floating cast of paid officials from the federal headquarters. All of them were dedicated people. However, they did not in any way represent a cross-section of the party. Just as important, all of them had joined the group as organizers and strategists, with not a policy specialist in the crowd.

The working group was equipped to handle packaging and marketing, but not the full range of product development. A political party distributes posters, advertisements, speeches; all of these rest on a substructure of ideas. In this last regard, the NDP spends millions on advertising and polling, but neglects basic research and development — the same sin the party often attributes to short-sighted corporations. The convention resolutions process is intended to put new ideas before the strategists, but the process is outdated and overloaded, and its importance to the strategy process is questionable.

The NDP system, where democratically approved ideas go nowhere, has little appeal for young idealists who want to change the world. Young people should serve as the party's early warning system. They see the effects of global industrial change on their own generation. Many of them, however, describe the culture of the party as alien, and are far more likely to spend time with issue groups. Peter Bleyer, a young sociologist who works full-time with a social action coalition, calls his years in the New Democratic Youth "one of the most boring activities I ever engaged in … It was a culture of insiders."

Bleyer says the NDP addresses voters as consumers and signs up volunteers to do grunt work, but will not learn from their experience and insights. "This process is a manipulative one. It doesn't educate people or bring them into debate or take what they say into account. There's a problem in pretending to engage people when you're not really doing it."[14]

At another level, the federal NDP has only minimal contact with Canada's universities and think tanks. At one time the NDP prided itself on its academic wing. The first president of the party, Michael Oliver, edited a book of essays on then-current political topics while he was in office. Over time, the party lost its cutting edge.

There are exceptions, where one or another expert keeps a circle of senior party people informed on aspects of social policy or aboriginal affairs. But in general, the NDP has become what scientist and former MP Howard McCurdy calls "intellectually thin."[15] No one proposes that professors should run the show, but most social democratic parties have a system for plugging in new research on key issues, such as economic growth or public-sector management. The academics of the League for Social Reconstruction wrote the first CCF manifesto based on their economic and political research. Sweden's Social Democrats, held up so often as a model by the NDP, governed for 20 years using the work of economists whose first report stood the Swedish party on its head.

Daniel Drache of York University has put together several anthologies of articles by left-wing academics — on trade, the economy, the workplace and Quebec independence. These works overflow with ideas that never engaged the NDP caucus or executive during the 1989–93 Parliament: on the role of governments and trade unions in restructuring the Canadian economy, the changing meaning of jobs and full employment for the individual worker, the need to prepare a social democratic response to Quebec independence. Drache complains that there is no route for new ideas to find their way into the NDP.

What is the relationship between policy and political fortunes? Once you've developed enough expertise, the leader and the MPs begin to feel comfortable with the issues, and they get better at talking about them ... For the Liberals, the Red Book represented a process of renewal — they actually sat down and said, If we come to power, what can we realistically do?

There's a very large policy community in Canada, and the NDP doesn't use it very well. They don't trust academics — I think they think we're jerks. We know a lot of things, but they don't take advantage of that, and they pay a terrible price. If you want to develop alternative policies that are really alternative and tough and credible, you have to reach out, and the NDP has a poor record of reaching out.[16]

One explanation for this rift with the intellectuals is that the NDP cannot tolerate a diversity of views. Academics, says John Richards of Simon Fraser University, are a "cheap date ... They love a forum, and they love to hear the sound of their own voices." In return, they demand some respect for freedom of debate, which Richards says is a low priority in the NDP.

James Laxer, who took part with Richards in the radical Waffle movement between 1969 and 1972, links the restrictions on debate in the party to the NDP's identity as a party under siege — small, vulnerable, and therefore paranoid. Others say the Waffle itself did permanent damage to the spirit of the NDP. Historian Desmond Morton says the Waffle's legacy "was a tendency to turn policy debate into a power play and to turn what I had joined as a 'society of friends' into a faction-ridden battlefield ... I mention the Waffle only because I think that it is a frightening and threatening memory for a party which cannot stand to tear itself apart again in a search for its own fresh definition."[17]

Whoever is to blame, the Waffle era left behind a memory of division and a vigilant core of mainstream party regulars ready to weed out dissent. Doug Coupar, who was still in high school when the Waffle was banned in Ontario, says the expulsion "drove out hundreds if not thousands of people who should be in the NDP and supporting the NDP financially. A leadership style that says consensus must triumph over all leads to an absolute loss of brainpower."[18]

Until its financial and leadership crisis of 1994, the party has continued to hold policy conventions every two years. Officially, they are the showpiece of party democracy, and provide an outlet for party members to shape policy in their own areas of interest. "Policy is determined democratically at biennial conventions by votes after debate, and in between conventions by elected councils. The party's support comes from the grass roots in a way that no other party can claim."[19]

But critics point out that a committee chosen by convention organizers and its own chair chooses the resolutions to be debated. In 1983, local associations and labour submitted 500 resolutions; 41 made it to the floor. In this way, the party avoids controversy and embarrassment. "The Conservatives deal with this problem by having no policy conventions, the Liberals have policy conventions but forget the resolutions once the conventions are over, and the NDP leadership makes sure it gets the resolutions it wants."[20]

In important cases, resolutions are derailed before they reach convention. In 1983, provincial leaders Allan Blakeney and Grant Notley, working with a group of thinkers including John Richards, produced a statement on new directions for the NDP. The federal leader's office put the document through the brokering mill to prevent public argument — that is, they shopped it around to provincial leaders and top labour people — and served the product to the party convention on a take-it-or-leave-it basis. Richards wrote: "The resulting 'cut and paste' manifesto lacked the legitimacy it would have enjoyed had it emerged as the result of open debate on the convention floor."[21] The document was soon forgotten.

Episodes like this at the federal and provincial levels have spawned a stream of critical writing on the NDP as the No Dissent Party.[22] Social activists are notoriously hard to please, of course; even a process-oriented organization like the National Action Committee on the Status of Women, which takes great pains to keep its agenda open, comes under attack for élite and "male" practices.[23] But in the NDP, there is a widespread view that the No-Dissent regime has won permanent victory and killed the party's idealistic roots. The 1989 convention debate on Canada's Constitution went as smoothly as a pro wrestling match, as did a similar debate in 1991. The current leaders in the two largest provincial sections, Mike Harcourt and Roy Romanow, waltzed into their jobs unopposed. Even former federal secretary Bill Knight, "the establishment czar of all time," yearns for the days when the membership would rise up and when controversies "walked through walls" despite the fixers and brokers.[24]

A restless, unfocused desire in the party for more democracy led several of the 1989 leadership candidates to promise reform, but change has been slow under Audrey McLaughlin. Former MP John Brewin says most NDP meetings still resemble medieval church services, with the priests at the front and the peasants going through the motions on the floor. Before the party cancelled the 1994 convention, organizers were considering the creation of a new debate facilitation committee that would give all points of view a chance to speak.

A more democratic convention process may make for a happier and more active membership; it may or may not encourage the development of useful ideas, or the integration of policies into the social democratic platform. Without dismissing the importance of conventions, it seems clear that ideas must also proceed from other channels. The party must organize smaller forums and meetings, forget the political blood test, and invite non-NDP experts to present alternatives to key party people. Ed Broadbent's circle made a gesture in the 1980s with a seminar by satellite, "Canada 2000," laughingly remembered as "Canada 200,000" because of its cost. The reports it is said to have produced are long out of circulation. In 1990, policy director Brian McKee sent out a questionnaire on the economy to 1,000 teachers and policy specialists and got 100 responses, but he had no resources for follow-up or discussion. Not even the academic public-opinion experts have been tapped for their ideas, despite the party's obvious need to do good, accurate polling.

Do all the NDP's problems arise from a rigid, cliquish executive style? Alan Whitehorn, a close academic observer of the NDP, writes that this view is "simplistic, repetitive, and one-sided."[25] In fact, in looking at the federal NDP's resistance to new ideas, one could make the argument that the party is not rigid enough or disciplined enough in organizing its resources.

As in the lives of most individuals, the NDP's anxieties about trivia have put important long-term problems on hold indefinitely. MPs' offices and party offices concern themselves with citizen complaints and inquiries. In the 1988–93 Parliament, the now-defunct NDP research unit spent its time translating government decisions and reports into plain language, writing MPs' questions for Question Period, and gathering political input from issue groups. The leader's advisers, with no academic or policy background, took responsibility for defining the NDP response to issues, but almost always in a climate of panic. The party office, meanwhile, hired organizer after organizer as the election approached, but kept the single policy officer at an intermediate level.

There was rarely time to think, given the often false urgency of preparing for the next vote or club luncheon speech. Now there is time. If it is to emerge again as a serious force, the NDP must take on the problem of how to absorb new ideas — how to attract young idealists, offer some democratic outlet for activists, and rise above beer parlour debate by funding some serious, hard-headed economic research and analysis.

In the last year before the election, a subcommittee of the election planning group developed the 60-page Jobs Plan. The Plan was mostly a back-room product, and somewhat limited in scope. Even so, the energy it tapped suggested the presence of a tremendous reservoir of intelligence and ideas in the party and the community.

The federal NDP will face a final, and perhaps fatal hurdle in any search for a fresh self-definition. Even if it had won 50 seats in 1993, it would still remain a weak, dependent extension of the larger provincial sections. In British Columbia, Saskatchewan and Manitoba, these sections control head offices larger than the federal headquarters. Some Western members view the federal party as a nuisance and resist any statement or action at the federal level that rubs up against provincial electoral priorities.

Until fairly recently, more than 70 per cent of the 150 Federal Council members attended as nominees of the provinces or territories. The 1991 convention added 56 new councillors, mostly from federal ridings. However, in the view of the federal staff who organized the change, the heavyweights on Council still represent regional interests — including provincial presidents, secretaries and leaders.

The provincial sections sign up the members and keep the membership lists. They share the lists with Ottawa when and if they want to. (Combined provincial membership lists in spring 1994 added up to about 110,000 names. This figure may overstate the real membership; some sections keep not-paid-up members on their lists for up to three years.)

Provincial offices also take in most of the cash from party donors. The two levels have worked out a formula for an automatic split, but provincial sections often fall behind in sending money to Ottawa. When Marion Dewar became federal president in 1985, she found seven provinces in arrears, which hurt the federal party's ability to pay staff and organize meetings.

The party was not financed as most New Democrats thought it was, with 15 per cent of federal donations going to federal office. The provinces chose never to pay. It embarrasses me to say this, but we used to have fire sales of the provinces' debt. If British Columbia owed us $100,000 because they'd had an election, then to coerce them into paying something we'd offer them a 2-for-1 deal and let them pay $50,000. It seemed so ridiculous, although everybody else on the executive thought it was quite all right and quite serious.

When I did an analysis of what was happening, I realized that we don't have a federal party.[26]

The provincial offices house the field organizers and co-ordinate much of the federal election advertising and federal worker training. In other words, federal MPs depend on the goodwill of the provincial party to hang on to their jobs. Nelson Riis calls the NDP "a collection of provincial organizations whose first thought is not the federal party and often not Canada." There is pressure on MPs to ignore the national mood if the interest of a provincial NDP regime is at stake. When the B.C. NDP government announced the plan to open Clayoquot Sound for logging, New Democrats across Canada who opposed the decision were left without a voice. Riis says he and his colleagues were "muzzled."

Here we are trying to set up a pan-Canadian party based on an organization of people whose first priority is provincial. No wonder we're having trouble. The minute a provincial leader takes a position on anything, there's a feeling that we have to fall in and support that, no matter how parochial it is.

We have to develop a structure where we can have federal positions that may conflict from time to time with a provincial position. Philosophically we should be fine, but on policy issues we have to be prepared to differ.[27]

The provincial parties hold a controlling interest in the federal NDP. The two levels of the party have shared many victories and defeats. As matters stand in 1994, Roy Romanow, Mike Harcourt and Bob Rae have more power than anyone else over the development of any new federal consensus in the party. A rapid disentangling of the federal and provincial levels is not likely — unless the provinces walk away from the federal party, leaving organized labour to pick up the pieces. As long as the premiers (or future ex-premiers) hold the high cards, there will be pressure on the federal party to limit the scope of debate and experimentation.

The success of the NDP's rebuilding effort will depend partly on the next leader, and on her or his ability to balance provincial demands against the need to set a distinctive federal course. But it would be a mistake to invest too much hope in the coming change of leadership. Even a popular, politically savvy leader like Ed Broadbent could not remake the party working alone; neither could Audrey McLaughlin, despite the appeal of her program for change. The salvaging of the federal NDP must be undertaken as a collective effort by members, former members and future members, or it will not happen at all.

2

The Leadership

Broadbent's target was the welfare liberals who normally support the Liberal Party. His hope was that they would find a centrist NDP more attractive than a business-oriented Liberal Party. Consequently, Broadbent soft-pedalled public references to democratic socialism, and sought instead to portray New Democrats as the representatives of decent, caring Canadians.
— William Christian and Colin Campbell[1]

When the party faithful gather at the community hall, they experience a breathless moment as the Leader enters the room. They yearn for a glimpse of the authority that carried J.S. Woodsworth and Tommy Douglas into legend.

The handlers who work with politicians take a less reverent view. A noted pollster remarked that the difference between a bar of soap and a politician is that "soap doesn't talk."[2] When a provincial NDP leader grumbled about another change in his schedule, Audrey McLaughlin said grimly to him, "Don't fight it, Ray. We're just pieces of meat."

McLaughlin lived in the shadow of the party's previous leaders and of a thousand diverse and conflicting expectations. In an uneasy attempt at humour, she sometimes described herself as an entertainer in the show-biz world of politics: she was Ginger Rogers, who had to dance as fast as Fred Astaire, "except backwards and in high heels." Unfortunately, as a real entertainer at her first Parliamentary Press Gallery dinner in 1990 she flopped badly. The anecdotes and one-liners that had worked so well with her friends inspired whispers at the tables. The rumour of her embarrassment spread for weeks. The headline in the tabloid Ottawa *Sun* shouted "From hero to zero." The media were searching for something in McLaughlin that night: charisma, a hint of the heroic, the ability to fill the room with her presence ...

Audrey McLaughlin came late to politics, and even in front of the cameras she admitted her discomfort with the process. She resisted efforts to remake her image and personality, and shielded her family from the public eye. She wanted to remain Audrey the social worker: to listen, mediate and speak firmly for those who had no voice. Between 1989 and 1993, McLaughlin travelled widely. She spoke to audiences and talked to reporters in every region. In Ottawa, she took part in countless Question Periods and corridor scrums. She posed for magazine covers and co-wrote a book about herself. The party launched and re-launched her.

When the NDP was popular, the polls showed that voters saw McLaughlin as a caring, competent person. But more detailed research identified this as hope, projection, part of a search for a mother figure. To express their feelings about Mother Audrey, people at focus groups chose photographic images of women with babies, women with old people, a pair of hands cupped to hold the planet Earth.

As McLaughlin's term in office wore on, the public grew tired of waiting, and she became less popular. The leader's team could not communicate her personality or her humanness. Most Canadians knew what she was, but not who she was.

Political scientist Jill Vickers says that "the federal party has always been weak, and got the leaders that provincial sections thought it deserved."[3] The leadership of the federal party has always changed hands against a background of classic Canadian ambivalence. Tommy Douglas came aboard to fill a vacuum. When David Lewis's turn came, he almost lost to a 29-year-old unknown. Ed Broadbent was ready to leave politics; he was called back, and won a lukewarm mandate.

Each of these leaders, however, quickly graduated to the NDP hall of fame. NDP speakers and agitators invoke their names in defence of the status quo or when they seek to overthrow it. As the party's supporters crept away in the twilight of the 1993 campaign, Audrey McLaughlin made urgent appeals to the memories of Tommy Douglas, David Lewis, Stanley Knowles and Agnes Macphail.

Above all, Tommy Douglas: in life a cheery, irreverent little man, he now looms over the NDP as its patron saint. Douglas represents the myth of the party's origins early in the 20th century. As a father of medicare, his name is linked to the most reliable of NDP campaign issues.[4] As an elder statesman, Douglas influenced the party until his

death in the mid-1980s, and many relatively young people still remember him with awe. He could generate euphoria in almost any
crowd. At his best, said Stephen Lewis, he could touch the hearts of
his listeners and clarify their understanding in the same moment. "It
was a great, compelling gift."[5]

When the federal NDP gathered for its convention in Regina in
1983, it stood low in the polls. Party leader Ed Broadbent faced deep
splits over the Constitution and energy resources. Douglas, then 79
and in poor health, was wheeled up to the stage in a golf cart, and
spoke for an hour. He entreated the party to remember its roots and
unite.

Nothing in the text of the speech explains the crowd's reaction. A
quick paraphrase might go, "Fight on, fight on, fight on, fight on."
But the force of Douglas's rhetoric and his reputation moved his
audience to shouts, tears and standing ovations of up to 10 minutes.
Some in the audience later gave him credit for saving the party with
one speech.

The legend of the fighting preacher obscures Douglas's record in
office. In the 1940s, he and his CCF provincial cabinet compromised
with the bond dealers and banks who held the mortgage on Saskatchewan. By spending carefully, they achieved the elimination of the
province's debt. It took 17 years from the date of their first election
before they introduced province-wide medicare.

Premier Douglas left the West to lead the federal NDP in permanent opposition. In the Ottawa of the 1960s, as in the 1930s, he was
a voice crying in the wilderness. There was no more need to compromise. The rhetoric of "Us against Them" was freed from the
complications of having to deal with the private sector. Douglas and
David Lewis raged against the corporate villains: the banks, polluters, gougers of consumers, oil companies selling off Canada's resources. Lewis, leading the party in 1972, built his campaign on the
phrase "corporate welfare bums." The NDP's role, Douglas said late
in his life, should be to win small victories for the weak, to "get back
a little of the fruit of people's labour and give them a chance to enjoy
it."[6]

Ed Broadbent, an auto worker's son with a doctorate in political
science, led the party from 1975 to 1989. Measured by the opinion
polls, he was the most popular NDP leader ever. He came to know
the party inside out; it can also be argued that he failed to convert
the New Democratic Party to his views.

With his crooked teeth, a voice that soared too high and a closetful of corduroy, Broadbent's potential as a charismatic leader appeared doubtful at first. However, he had the support of both Douglas and Lewis. His main rival for the leadership, British Columbia MLA Rosemary Brown, launched her campaign with a promise to make the party more open and democratic. Brown's opponents denounced this as an attack on the revered leaders, and her campaign faltered. All the same, it took Broadbent four ballots to secure his victory.[7]

He took charge of a growing pool of financial resources provided by the House of Commons. Instead of depending on green assistants as Douglas had, Broadbent acquired a team of researchers and strategists led by a principal secretary, a person of mature political judgement who became a power in his own right. Parliament had put this team under the control of the leader, not the party or caucus, and it worked to promote the leader's interests. The research section, for example, spent much of its time refining the leader's parliamentary questions rather than examining long-term trends and issues.

As federal leader, Broadbent faced other powers within the party, above all Allan Blakeney, the veteran Saskatchewan politician who opposed the federal line on energy policy and then on the Canadian Constitution. In 1981, Broadbent made a remarkable solo decision to endorse the Trudeau patriation package and earned the wrath of many Western party members. Blakeney, Lorne Nystrom and their allies took to the microphones at the 1981 federal convention to ask the party to overrule the federal leader. Broadbent was forced to enlist the patriarchs, Douglas, Lewis and Knowles, to win the convention back.

Nystrom recalls that a fellow Saskatchewan dissident, MP Doug Anguish, later conceived of a plan to "Clark" the party leader. Anguish wanted to stand for the leadership at the 1983 convention; even if he won 30 per cent of the vote, he reasoned, Broadbent would be forced to resign, just as Joe Clark of the Conservatives had in similar circumstances. Anguish's colleagues, however, persuaded him to back off.[8]

Broadbent's friends and colleagues from university days were scattered throughout the senior levels of the NDP. At the time when the party sank to 9 per cent in the polls in late 1983, two of them occupied the positions of federal president and federal secretary. As Desmond Morton has related, Terry Grier and Gerald Caplan convinced the executive to finance a detailed opinion survey to be followed up by a media campaign. Together with Broadbent, they worked to focus the party's message and win back traditional support.

The poll, the first detailed survey to be carried out by the NDP, showed that people distrusted New Democrats as economic managers but identified the party with "the little guy." The pollster suggested that the party work on its economic credibility, but Caplan and Grier disagreed, choosing instead to play to the party's strength. Soon Broadbent learned to tie every sound bite to "standing up for ordinary Canadians."[9]

From this point on, the NDP (like other parties) made routine use of polls to define the "language," or stock phrases, that would appear in every speech and fundraising letter. The party accepted the conventional advertising wisdom that only countless repetitions of the magic words will get the party's message across to the public. Like an actor doing endless takes of a TV commercial, the leader must devour the same plate of cold noodles over and over, without losing his or her enthusiasm.

The 1984 election gave the NDP a chance to test this approach. With Pierre Trudeau's departure from the Liberal Party and the rise of corporate lawyer John Turner, it should have been a promising time for the NDP. But North America had lost its economic supremacy in the mid-1970s and plunged into recession in 1981. A rising chorus on the right blamed social programs, unions and big government. By 1984, Americans were preparing to re-elect the anti-union, anti-welfare populist Ronald Reagan. Gerald Caplan warned that the media had lost interest in the NDP, that they saw a party "fighting for a better yesterday."[10]

The campaign combined "standing up for ordinary Canadians" (a.k.a. "people like you") with a focus on Broadbent as the bearer of the message. In this verson of "Us and Them," "Us" were the over-taxed and overextended. "Them" were the rich investors and corporations who had made money in a jobless recovery and avoided taxes, as well as the politicians who protected them. Canadians were losing faith in their political leaders — a trend that would continue through to the 1990s — and some voters turned to Honest Ed Broadbent for the answer. He blasted his two opponents, John Turner and Brian Mulroney, as "the Bobbsey twins of Bay Street," and won back some left-leaning liberals. On election day 1984, the party collected 18 per cent of the popular vote and 30 seats, and staved off the disaster that had loomed a few months earlier.

The 1984 campaign produced two important results. First, it entrenched the use of polling as a guide to strategy. Call it science or voodoo, the polls gave non-elected NDP strategists a big boost in power relative to backbench MPs and other traditional representatives of the grass roots.

For the next several years, the polls dictated that NDP spokespeople should avoid economic issues if they had a choice. If they talked about the deficit or interest rates, TV viewers would be sceptical about what they had to say. The party leader and MPs should use their precious seconds on the TV news to show where the NDP reflected the majority view — on "standing up for ordinary Canadians," fair taxes, medicare and later, the environment. The NDP, as a modest third party, could only hope that its best issues stayed in the news. If the media reported on fair taxes, the NDP would be in the story. If the news priorities shifted — say, to economic management or the Constitution — the NDP might appear to have nothing credible to say.

The 1984 campaign also confirmed the NDP as Ed Broadbent's party. The campaign built around the leader saved many members of Parliament their seats, and they owed him a personal debt. Broadbent grew immensely popular with the public and reflected credit on everyone. The party granted him wide latitude on issues and he used it to distance himself, for example, from the party's official position on abandoning NATO. By the time he stepped aside, all but 3 of 42 MPs had come to Ottawa under his leadership. They would owe no favours to any new leader.

Over time, Broadbent refined his style and grew into the job. He had a wide grasp of issues and political ideas. He developed his skill for horse-trading with the labour leaders and regional barons who ran the party. More subtly, he learned the most human art of leadership: to win loyalty by making people feel important.

At the 1987 Alberta provincial convention in Calgary, Broadbent made his pitch to the 16-member provincial caucus in a breakaway room off a back corridor. In earnest and patient tones he explained to the MLAs why they must support the Meech Lake Accord. The fate of the country, he said, lay in their hands. The MLAs stared at their laps and shuffled their feet. The accord made a tempting target in Alberta, where many centre-left voters viewed it as a sop to Quebec and a sellout to reactionary premiers. However, the MLAs raised no murmur of protest, and they later voted in the legislature as Ed had asked them to.

Two hours after this meeting, Broadbent the charismatic leader sailed into the convention hall with music blaring. The militants who had poured their hearts and their energy into the party rose to their feet and cheered. It was Broadbent's first official appearance in Calgary in half a dozen years. He half-jogged up the aisle, read his speech, and showboated for the exit; with a scattering of handshakes, he was gone.

For a year or two Broadbent was the most popular leader in the country. The strategy of finding areas of majority discontent and turning them into populist causes was paying off. At the same time, the other major party leaders, Mulroney and Turner, were distinctly unpopular. Through early 1987, the NDP sailed along at over 40 per cent in the polls, with a substantial lead over the Liberals and Conservatives.

Photos of Broadbent in his prime show him smiling, relaxed, jacket slung casually over his shoulder, the model of strength and good humour. He and his aides, especially press secretary Peter O'Malley, had worked hard to improve Broadbent's image. "Just as he had learned to change his tailoring and to fix the gap in his teeth, he learned to modulate his voice."[11]

He won increasing coverage in the media. From 1984 to 1988, the NDP had almost as many MPs as the Liberals, and as Broadbent and his team hammered away in the Commons, some reporters began to treat them as the real Opposition, and possibly the next government. But the breakthrough never came.

The NDP entered the 1988 campaign with confidence. It stood at about 30 per cent in the polls, in a three-way tie with the Liberals and Conservatives. The party planned a replay of "ordinary Canadians," with Broadbent front and centre. In one NDP television advertisement, an old man assured a child that Ed Broadbent would make corporate polluters clean up the environment. A more upbeat ad showed actors dressed as bus drivers shouting "Ed Broadbent!" and making thumbs-up signs.

The NDP plan, however, ran afoul of the free trade issue, one of those rare "accidental outbreaks of politics … in this age of tightly scripted, media-driven election campaigns."[12] Liberal leader John Turner plunged into "the crusade of a lifetime" and a daily bath in the media spotlight. Broadbent addressed the trade deal in his speeches, but the NDP high command shied away from attacking the deal in television ads or media events. On Sundays, when the tour and communications crews met in an abandoned penthouse restaurant high above Ottawa, pollster Vic Fingerhut from Washington huffed and puffed over the week's losses, and then warned that any mention of the trade issue threw votes to the Liberals. "You've gotta stick to the populist stuff," he said. "Bay Street, Main Street, that stuff."

The year 1988 marked the climax of leadership politics. Everything rested on Broadbent's shoulders. The party needed him everywhere at once; the campaign team shipped him from Timmins to Edmonton to Saint John. Day by day he grew more weary.

In Chicoutimi, in 1988, we were the strongest party in terms of members. We had 2,000 members across the Saguenay region, and hoped to pick up one or two ridings. We were raising money, we had a hundred volunteers, and they all came to the Chicoutimi committee room to watch the debate on TV. They'd all heard about Ed Broadbent, they wanted to see him on the screen. Here was their champion.

Ed says something to Brian Mulroney about François Mitterrand being against free trade. Mulroney denied it: "Mitterrand n'a jamais dit ça." "Ah, vraiment?" Ed said. "C'est dommage." ["Really? Oh, that's too bad."] I watched, and there was a visible sag in the room, and after that people were just not into it. They started talking, having beers ... Ed did a great job, but he hadn't practised and he wasn't prepared for a debate in French. We'd been raising a thousand dollars a week — it fell to a hundred and fifty.[13]

In the English debate, Broadbent got tangled up on the NATO issue. The TV networks awarded Turner the winning 10-second clip. The NDP campaign was going sour. Staff on the leader's tour feuded and rewrote each other's work. The thematic unity of the campaign dissolved, followed by its creativity. The central strategy group considered sending Broadbent to Wall Street in New York for a pitch against corporate evil; he ended up posing in front of a bank machine on Bay Street in Toronto, since it was Saturday and banking offices were closed.

The NDP dropped to 20 per cent and a distant third by voting day. Afterwards, prominent critics such as Robert White of the Auto Workers and Gerard Docquier of the Steelworkers complained that Broadbent had avoided labour issues and labour events in an effort to take votes from the political centre. Fingers pointed to the central strategists — Bill Knight, George Nakitsas, Robin Sears — the men who had interpreted the polls, and who had met on Saturday nights to plan the agendas (and as much as possible the outcomes) of the larger Sunday meetings.

White's letter to Broadbent, which he later published as a magazine article, signalled trouble for the NDP, and the beginnings of a rift between the party and the most powerful man in Canadian labour.

> I can tell you that I've never seen such a level of disappointment and anger among our activists, "There is a common thread in the frustration, and that is that the NDP, our party, never really came to grips with the importance of free trade, were scared of it as an issue ... Why did our party not understand the emotions of people who were concerned about this new direction of the Mulroney government? I think we believed our pollsters, who convinced us that on economic issues the NDP doesn't do well. This was not an economic issue only, it was much deeper than that. We will not have, in the near future, another issue like free trade where there will be so much unanimity in the labour movement.[14]

Bill Knight resigned as federal secretary a few weeks after the election. In March of 1989, Broadbent announced his intention to resign as leader.

Broadbent's career shows the limits on the power of an NDP leader. He came to wear the stamp of the party, rather than imposing his stamp on it. An academic, a thinker, he made his name as "Honest Ed," the pal of ordinary Canadians. "While he was regarded as being the most 'likeable' and 'trustworthy,' he was less highly rated on questions of competence and ideas."[15]

Along the way, Broadbent left behind his ambition to reshape the party's economic outlook. As a rookie MP in 1968, he argued that the welfare-state concerns of the NDP, such as pensions, housing and regional development, could just as soon be handled by the Liberals. He wanted social democrats to go further, to talk about changing the way the workplace was run. He wanted to see the gradual takeover of industry by working people, "chipping away at the capitalist right of property ownership."[16]

Some older MPs such as Tommy Douglas encouraged him, but Broadbent ran into a wall of indifference and hostility from trade union leaders. Worker control and worker ownership, they said, would blur the lines of responsibility and power in the workplace. Giving responsibility to workers would open up new channels between workers and management, and threaten the role of union representatives. Broadbent later discussed this problem with his European colleagues, and came to accept the idea that no social democratic party can stray too far from the ideas of its trade union allies.

Many critics, left and right, have said the NDP's economic policies stagnated under Broadbent, that he defended a fading world of subsidies, state ownership and increased government spending.[17] In the early 1980s, his senior staff, especially research director James Laxer, grew impatient. They decided that Broadbent must "say something real" on the economy. In the fall of 1982, Broadbent broke his silence on the federal deficit. In a key speech in Hamilton, he floated the idea of a new economic program for the NDP, including investment in industry and increased taxes for high-income earners. It could all be done, he said, without increasing the federal deficit. For many in the party, even this implied criticism of the deficit was too strong. They associated deficit restraint with conservatism, and higher deficits with progressive ideas. They began to complain to the leader's office.

> First of all, Richard Gwynn [of The Toronto Star] wrote a column saying this was a great and heroic new beginning for Canadian social democracy. That was a bad thing. Ed phoned Richard and insisted that this was not a new beginning, that we weren't doing anything exciting.
>
> Dennis McDermott, who was the president of the CLC, told Ed that he didn't have any problems with the speech. But the serious decision-making level of the CLC, the bureaucratic level, was not happy. We began to hear criticism on Parliament Hill through the grapevine. Then this was leaked to the press, that people in the trade unions weren't happy. The pressure built up, until by the beginning of 1983 Ed was convinced this was the biggest political error he'd ever made. He reversed himself, and called for an enlarged deficit.[18]

The reaction by orthodox New Democrats to Broadbent's statement, coupled with the polls that advised the NDP to avoid the subject of economic management, entrenched the party's reliance on social policy and equality issues. As a predictable result, party activists lost touch with economic questions. Most New Democrats were unprepared to debate free trade at the local level when it emerged as the main issue of the 1988 campaign.

Broadbent also failed, despite intensive work, to establish the NDP in Quebec. Broadbent spoke fluent, if heavily-accented French; he developed personal ties with Québécois social democrats and grew to appreciate the deep roots of Quebec nationalism. After 1984, he gave his Quebec-born assistant George Nakitsas the time and resources to recruit talent, and support for the federal NDP grew rapidly. However, the resulting structure in Quebec was rickety and lacked legitimate home-grown leadership. Nakitsas, complained one important group of Quebec nationalists in the party, "imposed his personnel and his vision of things, and comported himself like a general in occupied territory."[19] With Broadbent's departure in 1989 and the federal party's decision to place new conditions on its support for the Meech Lake Accord, the NDP in Quebec fell apart. Staff in the new leader's office came to refer to the Quebec NDP as the "Club Bon Voyage."

When Broadbent retired, the federal NDP was still feeble in the Atlantic region and Quebec, still dependent on gaps in the Liberal Party for its electoral successes elsewhere. It maintained some strength in the polls, but many members and observers felt that the party had gone stale. Columnist Geoffrey Stevens wrote, "The New Democratic Party ... lacks direction, purpose, passion. It no longer knows what it stands for, whom it speaks for, or where it wants to go."[20] The NDP, in the harsh judgement of another journalist, was a moribund party that nobody wanted to lead.[21]

Broadbent had not groomed a successor. After he announced his plans to step down, the party's most prominent figures counted themselves out one by one. It was like 1960 again, and the podium waited, but the new Tommy Douglas did not step forward.

Political scientists Alan Whitehorn and Keith Archer had asked delegates from the previous NDP convention about their choices for leadership. Auto Workers president Robert White topped the poll, followed by former party president Marion Dewar, MPs Lorne Nystrom and Nelson Riis, former Ontario leader Stephen Lewis, and Nova Scotia leader Alexa McDonough.[22] They all declined the federal leadership for personal or professional reasons, as did Saskatchewan leader Roy Romanow (who stood an excellent chance of winning the next provincial election) and former Manitoba premier Ed Schreyer.

Some in the media linked this reluctance to New Democrat worries about the Liberal leadership. Jean Chrétien appeared likely to win the upcoming Liberal leadership contest, and it was said that many New Democrats feared disaster against Chrétien. According to this school of thought inside the party, said *The Edmonton Journal*, "The NDP might as well fold its tent now, pick an interim leader, and start planning for a post-Chrétien future."[23]

By mid-summer, six lesser-known candidates had come forward. Four were seasoned MPs, competent and articulate in English but generally unknown to the public. One was a bilingual schoolteacher with a utopian agenda. The sixth candidate, and the only woman in the race, was Audrey McLaughlin. She had been elected from the Yukon just two years before, but was already the NDP caucus chair. Her fellow MPs knew her as a friendly, unassuming person, someone with her feet on the ground.

In the absence of more high-profile candidates, McLaughlin picked up support quickly from the caucus and caucus staff. John Brewin of Victoria came to McLaughlin after Alexa McDonough bowed out; Joy Langan from Coquitlam gave up waiting for Dave Barrett to enter. Nelson Riis, the NDP House Leader, liked McLaughlin's lack of obligations to groups or factions. "I had a feeling that the party needed a real housecleaning and that we were so out of step with reality ... She was new, refreshing, and I also liked the fact that she happened to be a woman, and it would be useful for the party to be able to lead the way on that." [24]

McLaughlin gave the first news conference of her life the day she kicked off her leadership campaign. With less than two years' experience in Parliament, she still had the rough edges of the single mother who had worked her way through college. Her introductory leaflet described her as a community worker and as "The Voice of Tomorrow." After Rosemary Brown's experience in 1975, McLaughlin knew enough to heap praise on the departing leader, but she also promised an "alternative approach."

"The process begins by changing who defines the problems and who establishes the priorities. If you ask an aboriginal person or a struggling farmer to define the problems and priorities I guarantee you're going to get a different answer than if you ask the president of a bank or the head of a U.S. multi-national."[25]

A week after McLaughlin's entry, Auto Workers president Robert White disclosed that he was "deeply troubled" by the calibre of candidates in the race. "A strong leader doesn't guarantee success, but a weak leader guarantees failure," he told a union conference at Port Elgin. He also confirmed that he would not run for the party leadership. This, he said, was "a lifetime decision."[26]

The candidates went to local barbecues, and then began a series of leadership debates in August; the pundits declared themselves underwhelmed by the personalities and the debates. Party heavyweights still searched for a superstar. The public forums, *The Toronto Star* reported, were "little more than a sideshow to the frantic telephone appeals."[27]

In September, Ontario NDP leader Bob Rae considered a run. Ontario labour had decided, after holding a forum for the declared candidates, that Rae was their only hope. Steelworkers leaders had hoped to endorse McLaughlin, but "she didn't deliver. There was no substance. She was vacuous."[28]

Rae, by contrast, had an expert grasp of the economy and the Constitution, and spoke brilliantly in English or French. He had the backing of Saskatchewan godfather Allan Blakeney, prominent Ontario labour leaders and the Steelworkers organization, and the surviving New Democrats in Quebec. Rae's provincial caucus waited, some with joyful anticipation, for him to announce. But in the end he decided to stay put in Toronto. Strategists in other camps reported that Rae's people had polled Western delegates and found too much doubt there to assure him a victory.

While Rae pondered, Dave Barrett jumped in. Finally, the NDP had a star leadership candidate with a national profile, a politician with 15 years of experience as leader of the powerful B.C. party, including three years as premier.

Barrett offered a clear alternative to McLaughlin. If the Yukon MP stood for a process-oriented "new politics," Barrett represented a classic populist style. He was a fine improvising orator, a deft negotiator, a meeter and greeter. He combined a detailed knowledge of government with a delight in raising hell: on the day of his announcement he said the party had spent too much time on Quebec, and ruffled all the editorial and NDP feathers in French Canada.

The former B.C. premier had charisma behind the scenes, along with an unpredictable streak. Barrett liked to trust the spirit of the moment. Impatient with agendas, he would barge into a meeting, seize control, and share whatever master plan had come to him in the shower or the elevator. His joy infected everyone, even experienced politicians, although the rash usually faded when he left the room. None of this survived on paper, since Barrett objected to written minutes.

At the 1989 leadership convention, Barrett won a promise of support from fellow candidate Simon de Jong in a locked room, not guessing that de Jong wore a CBC television microphone that he had forgotten to disconnect. The Regina MP defected to McLaughlin a few minutes later. Coming as it did before an audience of millions, de Jong's flip-flop subjected him to endless scorn. However, his agonized "What have I done?" typified the second thoughts of many people seduced by Dave Barrett.

Barrett brought passion and eloquence to any point of view. He would stand up to address the federal caucus (the only MP to do so) and say, "We have three things to consider in this debate, and they are politics, politics, and politics," or, "I have spoken many times on this issue, on both sides and right up the middle." In general, though, Barrett's convictions led him back to "Us and Them": an opposition to corporate abuses, and a sentimental support for the struggles of working people and the poor. Barrett's side in 1989 included women and members of B.C.'s South Asian communities, but his core support among resource industry workers and wheat farmers represented a traditional NDP "Us." I attended the leadership convention as a delegate from Calgary Centre, and when I moved from Ian Waddell to McLaughlin on the second ballot, a female trade union employee shouted at me, "Can you imagine *her* addressing a bunch of miners in Temiskaming? Can you imagine them getting up and cheering for her the way they would for Dave? Who does Audrey have on her side, anyway? A bunch of yuppie white wine drinkers!"

McLaughlin defeated Barrett on the fourth ballot of the convention by 1,316 votes to 1,072. Barrett's backers were crushed. What bribes had this untried woman used to lure delegates? In a hotel lobby, a Barrett supporter snarled at me, "Well, I hope you get whatever it is they promised you."

It helped McLaughlin that she received endorsements from Robert White and from Steelworkers director Leo Gerard at the leadership convention. But it also helped that Barrett's camp consistently underestimated the McLaughlin team. A McLaughlin organizer recalls: "Barrett's people thought Audrey would fall apart in the bear-pit session. When she passed that, they said she would give a terrible speech. She did all right. Barrett's people went out to party after the speeches, and 35 of us sat up and planned voting day."[29] In particular, McLaughlin had the computer tracking system of the David Gotthilf, soon to become the federal party's pollster. From early in the campaign, Gotthilf was able to pinpoint McLaughlin's support and suggest strategies for winning over delegates through telephone campaigning and on the convention floor.

Here is what McLaughlin promised: an orthodox approach to NDP policy, but a radical redefinition of how the NDP operated. On the policy side, McLaughlin showed a special interest in equality issues such as reproductive choice, racial equality, gay rights and aboriginal claims. For the most part however, she embraced the party's "reject and preserve" agenda in a traditional way. The NDP must reject the corporate-driven economic trends of the 1980s and preserve Canada's social safety net. "No more post office closings. No more VIA Rail abandonments. No more nuclear reactors."[30] Nobody should be forced to relocate. She wanted jobs for young people in their own communities, she told leadership convention delegates, jobs on the family farm, jobs in in mining towns and fishing villages. "The day after the next election, I will let Washington know the trade deal is off."[31]

On the question of process, McLaughlin promised a bold new direction. "We must practice in our own party what we seek in Canada — power sharing. Especially the inclusion of all those who have been left out of Canada."[32] Ordinary Canadians would no longer be spectators, and no longer victims; they would join a rising culture of popular activity and be enhanced in dignity and pride. *"My kind of leadership listens and consults. I've seen countless examples where decisions were made for people without asking them what they needed ... The result, invariably, is disaster."* The party would ensure it was a serious contender in the next election by joining with labour and social action groups and "encouraging real democracy in society."[33]

For many supporters, especially the women, McLaughlin's victory at the 1989 convention signalled a new beginning. She embodied a hope that the New Democratic Party, now a generation old and showing severe signs of fatigue, could be transformed and renewed. "I felt like my heart was going to choke me," says Joy Langan. "There was such a thrill to have broken that barrier. But there was something else. A reporter asked me about Audrey's personal life, and I thought, I wonder if she even has a personal life? How much more can you give up than being an MP?"[34] Others like Nelson Riis stewed about a possible split in the party, wondering if Barrett's supporters could ever whole-heartedly support the new leader. In the end, he says, despite Barrett's impeccable record of public support for the leader, the split did not heal.[35]

Audrey McLaughlin took on the leadership almost as a political newcomer. Tommy Douglas had 26 years of elected experience when he became leader; Ed Broadbent had 7 years; Audrey McLaughlin just over 2 years. Inexperienced as she was, she now undertook to redefine leadership. She was not going to be either an autocrat or a mouthpiece for handlers. She promised a new politics that would be, as one of her speechwriters said, "constructive, inclusive and honest. We were not going to oppose for the sake of opposing. Everybody would feel part of the process, new people taking part."

In order to put this project into effect, she had two options. She could set out to re-create what had become a party of organizers and strategists through reason and her own feminist example, or she could try to dominate and manipulate it into turning its back on domination and manipulation.

It would all be as easy as pushing a string.

3

In Search of Ms. McLaughlin

Women tend to listen, men tend to talk.
— Audrey McLaughlin[1]

It took four or five months for Audrey McLaughlin to get settled into her job. She hired two young men, Les Campbell and Michael Balagus, to run her office and advise her. Together, they agreed on a demanding program of speeches and visits across Canada, plus regular phone contact with 60 or more prominent New Democrats. Among these were the leading women in the party, such as Alexa McDonough in Nova Scotia, Elizabeth Weir in New Brunswick, and Ontario NDP president Julie Davis.

At first, McLaughlin enjoyed a flattering spate of media attention. "Her impish good looks are reminiscent of Audrey Hepburn, her political savvy of Margaret Thatcher and her listening skills of Lester Pearson," wrote the editor of *Homemaker's Magazine.* "Those who do know her say Audrey McLaughlin is the political messiah this country has been waiting for, the leader of the '90s."[2]

And then, to the disappointment of her supporters, she began to fade from view.

In many ways, I think Audrey did what she said she'd do. She went out and met with groups, no matter how small or large, in every region of the country. She tried to plug into the process many of the people who had never had the opportunity to talk to somebody in a position of leadership in a political party.

Obviously, that didn't do what she hoped it would. It didn't bring them to us in an electoral sense. It will take some analysis to understand what went on, and why it wasn't as exciting to Canadians as the delegates and the party thought it would be.[3]

I have put myself in an awkward position here, writing critically of a former boss. McLaughlin has shown personal strength in a trying situation; she was not the only cause, nor the main cause, of the NDP's 1993 defeat. But as someone who accepted payment to focus public attention on McLaughlin's "new politics," I will admit I never understood what she had in mind. She was a novice politician, sometimes willing, sometimes fearful, taking on too big a job.

My first conversation with Audrey McLaughlin came when she interviewed me for a speechwriting position. We sat on couches in her square, sunny office with two walls of windows overlooking the Ottawa River. I talked much and hastily. I did not get the job. I sensed a woman who was aloof beyond the normal reserve of a politician meeting a stranger. She seemed also to come quickly to firm judgements.

A year later, McLaughlin's chief assistant, Les Campbell, hired me to write reports on the politics of the Constitution. I moved into an alcove down the echoing corridor from the square, sunny office. In my glimpses of the leader, she seemed efficient, driven by her schedule, voracious in her demand for scripts and lines. My responsibilities were unclear; Lorne Nystrom, the party Constitution critic, regarded me as Campbell's spy. My memos disappeared into limbo, my newsletters into bureaucratic chaos. I soon moved to another building and into a job where I produced the one-page flyers and brochures the party calls "literature."

In summary, I experienced McLaughlin as personally distant, and her central operation as disorganized. These were not trivial problems, but another issue strikes me as more crucial to her leadership.

Somehow, the momentum that had brought her to power had vanished. As a worker on a smaller leadership campaign, I had seen an uprising of feminist, democratizing energy behind McLaughlin the candidate. However, I did not detect major changes in the party under McLaughlin the leader, either while I worked for her or afterwards, with the important exception of an affirmative action program for federal candidates. There was some broadening out of power at the élite level — for example, in election planning — but there was no stirring at the grass roots, no program to harness the strength and energy of the party in any new way.

I raised this point with her in March 1994. The woman who had told the 1989 NDP convention, "I want to change Canada; that's why I want to be prime minister," seemed baffled by my questions. She replied at length only on my fourth try.

IM: You had a lot of grass-roots support from people who saw you and other women saying, "Let's do something with this party, let's put our stamp on it" ... It's just difficult for me to apprehend how that wave worked its way through the system.

AM: Well, again, one is always being judged by a standard that no one can define, which I think you just proved. The difficulty is that you're being judged against a feeling. The only indices I can point to are the things I have tried to be consistent about. One: putting in the affirmative action policy, and that was not just related to women. Second: working with youth ... I'm the one who has fought for more money at the federal level. I'm the one who in this process is saying we'd better have youth with us going into the 21st century.

But how do you judge these things, except by electoral success? That's the harshness of politics. Everyone would say I'd done a wonderful job if we'd had at least one-third women in a caucus the same size or bigger [after the 1993 election]. Everything I've done would have been acknowledged as being great.

I can't give you any other indices. I don't know how other people would judge it, and I don't think they know, either.[4]

Who were McLaughlin's allies? Four women MPs, a few other prominent New Democrat women, her paid advisers ... After months of asking the question, my list remains very brief. Did she think the entire party would happily take up her agenda for change with a signal from the top? Did she think she could operate alone? Or did her leadership campaign platform simply express a passive preference, a wish that someday things might be different?

"She had very short experience in politics, and we just sort of threw her to the wolves," says Marion Dewar, a former party president and friend. "I feel guilty about my decision to get off the executive and just act as a personal support. Well, she didn't need people to help her feel good, she needed people to help her confront the politics. We popped her in there, and she had no constituency in the party."[5]

The world of party politics is still alien ground for most Canadian women. McLaughlin has described it in her book and her speeches to women as a zone of competition, aggression and male bonding. This male dominance goes largely unrecognized by men. In Canadian politics, as an example, a Conservative male mafia can humiliate and then banish a recently defeated woman prime minister, something that would be inconceivable with a male leader. Partly in response to the male system, Canadian women have built an extensive culture of their own. It confronts mainstream politics through a national movement for women's equality, by some standards the most multifaceted and durable movement of its kind.[6] It was at the community level of this movement, in the Yukon, that McLaughlin built an important part of her early political base.

Canadian feminists encounter some ironies in putting their theory into practice. They seek equality with men and an end to the stereotypes that have kept women in ghettos; at the same time, they build feminist solidarity very largely on generalizations about the special experience of women.[7] Judy Rebick, former president of the National Action Committee on the Status of Women, says women activists "don't want to work with men, because they think their issues will always get sidelined."[8] Audrey McLaughlin writes of "the traditional male definition of power" in terms of "coercion, power *over*; 'now that I have power, I can get my way; I can get people to do things my way.' Women tend to think of power in terms of responsibility."[9]

In its populist, activist form, Canadian feminism understandably takes on an "Us and Them" quality. It makes a poor fit with any mass political party that is trying to win votes from the male mainstream. McLaughlin broadened her "Us" to include all those who supported the movement for justice and equality. Predictably, she ran into criticism from two sides: from those who felt she had abandoned the women's agenda, and from those who still found her feminism heavy-handed.

McLaughlin's leadership victory followed several years of growing women's influence in the NDP. The party had elected its first woman president, Marion Dewar, in 1985. During the mid-80s it had also achieved gender parity on its executive, and became the first party to take a clear stand on the right of women to choose abortion. In the 1988 federal election, the New Democratic Party fielded 50 per cent of all women candidates, and elected five women to Parliament.[10] In organized labour, meanwhile, the growing influence of women had put issues like child care, pay equity and affirmative action at the centre of the bargaining table and the union convention.

History demanded more: in every industrial country, women in politics discussed the need to go beyond "women's issues" and confront the male bias in the economy and the state. Women must take more positions of leadership; but did this mean using male means to capture the male centre of power? When Ed Broadbent stepped aside, the New Democratic women MPs, provincial women MLAs and many women on party staff rallied around the only woman candidate running to succeed him. McLaughlin's double mission, says Marion Dewar, was to rescue power in the NDP from "the boys in the back rooms" and to touch the pulse of the country. "I saw a woman leader as somebody who could be practical about the economic changes, but not lose the vision about how people could participate."[11]

McLaughlin often spoke about sharing power and going beyond the élites. She praised the virtues of aboriginal culture and its reputation for granting a voice to everyone in the circle. Audrey McLaughlin "was absolutely passionate about the need to open up the process beyond the stuffed shirts," says Michael Balagus, McLaughlin's director of communications. "It was one of her strongest and deepest passions."[12] This passion for equality, says political scientist Jill Vickers, reflects the core values of feminism.

> The understanding of leadership from feminist culture is very different from what it is in male-stream or mainstream culture. The "leader" imposing her policy values on an organization is unacceptable; it's frowned on.
>
> The only acceptable face of leadership is as facilitation. That means attention to process, the dissolving of hierarchical structures so that more and more people can participate in decision-making ... That was a central theme, as I understood it, of what Audrey and people like Marion Dewar were arguing for the party.
>
> Now, I think they also assumed, probably incorrectly, that this would produce the right answer. That's one of the problems in feminist political analysis — the assumption that if we get the process right, we'll all agree on the answer.[13]

McLaughlin used a recorded theme song at the 1989 leadership convention called "Talkin' 'Bout a Revolution." She came from a grass-roots feminist movement which, in its own orbit, has transformed politics, although its vocabulary sets many NDP members' teeth on edge.

By force of numbers and argument, Canadian feminists have changed the culture of local social action groups working on issues such as the environment and community planning. They understand that activists can do more than lick stamps and post signs. They have redefined leadership and participation. They have encouraged people to broaden their skills. This is what the McLaughlin campaign promised the NDP: a chance to shed some of the mind-numbing, paramilitary character of political work.

The NDP, despite McLaughlin's victory, did not prove to be fertile ground for feminist transformation. Grass-roots feminist culture and partisan politics, it seems, are very hard to blend. The media still want star actors, conflict and bluster. The manoeuvring among parties encourages the players to hoard information and distrust their allies. McLaughlin's party still has a poor record of consulting with its members and the public, due partly to the supreme power vested in male provincial NDP leaders.

McLaughlin, attempting to develop leadership by facilitation, was in the wrong environment. There was no revolutionary energy among the MPs or party moguls to facilitate, and she declined to "impose her policy values." Political scientist Caroline Andrew suggests that New Democrat women lacked the "critical mass" to put a feminist program for change into effect. Scandinavian experience indicates that women need to hold at least a third of the effective leadership jobs in order to take a party in a new direction.[14] The NDP women had gender parity on the party and caucus executives, but the provincial premiers, the cabinet ministers, the caucus veterans and the strategists were overwhelmingly male.

Many of the promises McLaughlin made in her campaign — public accountability sessions, a Conference on Socialism in Canada, an outreach program, a political education program — went unfulfilled. The work of developing these ideas was never assigned. The resources available in the $2 million annual party budget and the $9 million caucus budget were never tapped.

John Brewin, a McLaughlin campaign supporter, says he does not recall any of her campaign proposals for reform coming before the caucus. Dick Proctor, who ran the party headquarters when McLaughlin assumed the leadership, says the NDP executive "talked a lot about doing more outreach to women's groups and to environmentalists and to young people, but there wasn't a coherent plan, with the exception of the search for candidates."

"Inclusiveness was very much a part of her approach, but I am hard pressed to remember specific things that came out. So how are

we going to make this party more inclusive? I don't really think there
was anything."[15]

Why did New Democrats choose McLaughlin to lead them? Nelson Riis, the caucus heavyweight, says it was time to choose a
woman. And McLaughlin was new on the federal scene, with no dues
owing to any section of the party. Michael Lewis of the powerful
Steelworkers union says the same thinking motivated him and his
colleagues at Steel. Marion Dewar raises the same point. "Audrey
McLaughlin didn't carry a lot of the baggage within the party of who
had organized with whom. I thought she would be able to bring this
party together. It didn't happen."[16]

In the absence of a candidate who had friends in every faction, the
party turned to the candidate who had the fewest enemies. Her
inexperience in television, leadership and management could even
be turned into an advantage at a time when the public hated politicians. McLaughlin was a non-politician, an ordinary Canadian, an
Abe Lincoln in from the backwoods.

Jill Vickers suggests that the NDP chose McLaughlin to be a
sacrifical lamb, as the Conservatives and other parties in trouble have
chosen women leaders. She would take the fall, says Vickers, with
cheerful grace. Any woman at the head of a minor party faced a
double disadvantage, but a politician like Alexa McDonough would
at least know the issues and have experience in keeping a divided
institution together. McLaughlin, fresh from the world of community
groups where everyone shares common, more easily defined goals,
faced a leap "as wide as the Grand Canyon."[17] Others disagree with
this thesis; they point to McLaughlin's proven competence as caucus
chair and the enthusiasm at the 1989 convention, the feeling that
history, for once, was on the side of the NDP.

In her speeches, McLaughlin laughed at the idea that politics had
been her long-term goal. To young people who dreamed of becoming
prime minister someday, her advice was "get a life." She told me
once that she was a bit like Pierre Trudeau. She had moved naturally
into public life after many careers. She had worked as a mother,
farmer, social worker and executive director in Ontario, as a teacher
in Africa, and as a community developer and consultant to aboriginal
groups in the Yukon. A middle-aged citizen of the world, she tried
to keep her job in perspective.

In her office, McLaughlin could be tough and rigid, and kept
squads of researchers and writers focused on her needs. With visitors,
she was attentive but brisk. With her confidants she could also play

the Mae West character, joking that men in Ottawa had nothing hard in their pants except their cellular phones.[18]

Often, though, her tough act seemed as hollow as the laugh she used when a reporter's question hit home. A part of her remained youthful and optimistic and ripe for disappointment. She appeared unable to adjust to the weight of the job, the formalities, the intrigue.

Her intermittent discomfort was so intense that some wondered why she stayed. This was complicated by a different issue, her feminist concern with process and power-sharing, which many men could not see as leadership at all.

"I don't know why somebody like that would go into politics in the first place," says a senior party official. "She's a loner. She doesn't enjoy the camaraderie of caucus. It seems painful to her ... I think she was talked into running for the leadership. She didn't grow with the job — in fact, she seemed to hate it."

Judy Rebick agrees. "I don't think she really enjoys being the leader of the party. She's a very private person, a very reserved person. It's visible that she doesn't enjoy it, so she's not as attractive as she could be as a leader."[19]

McLaughlin's book, *A Woman's Place*, hints at the conflict between her motivations and her fears. Coming out of the sombre, hard-working atmosphere of small-town Ontario, she had suffered isolation working at home in the complacent 1950s, and then repeated disappointment in her dealings with men. Always, she struggled for self-esteem, remembering the early lessons that "girls don't quite measure up,"[20] and the reporters' doubts about her leadership bid, the kind of doubts that "many women hear over and over again."[21]

Her unsureness came out in peculiar ways. Michael Balagus says she declined to hire staff who had served on her leadership campaign: "If they worked for me, they can't be very good."[22] In fact, after hosting a social hour for her leadership campaign workers in Ottawa, she never contacted them again. She was considerate in sending out thank-you cards and get-well notes, but she seemed reluctant to cultivate the loyalty of others face to face, to ask for personal favours, to make people feel good about themselves. Perhaps she reasoned that her colleagues and staff had joined the NDP to uphold certain principles and that no further encouragement was required.

McLaughlin named Nelson Riis, an early supporter, to act as deputy leader of the party. However, even he did not seem to have a special relationship with the leader. Riis was a respected parliamentarian and a media star. He worked faithfully for solidarity in caucus and as a negotiator with the government on matters of House business. He did nothing to promote a feminist redistribution of power, but he was like McLaughlin in some ways: a facilitator, without an extensive agenda of his own. McLaughlin's advisers treated Riis's shop as they did all other MPs' offices; that is, they ignored it and kept it in the dark.

McLaughlin spent much of her day in meetings or on the phone, but she never developed a trusted group of informal advisers. Early in her term, she tried to build a panel of key strategists, but she caved in to demands from around the party that she include every region and interest. The "Committee on What the Leader Should Do for Us" became unmanageable. "They were terrible meetings, and the thing died a slow and painful death."[23]

Why not a circle of women? Dewar brought together some NDP women from around Ottawa, but "they weren't honest meetings. They were for personal support, rather than saying, Audrey, you're losing the political support you got because you're getting wrong messages."[24]

"I've seen it numerous times in the NDP," says Judy Rebick, a long-time party activist. "People come together for conventions, and then their organization falls apart. A lot of those women had other priorities ... There are so few women at that level of leadership. I found that when I was in the referendum campaign. For Audrey to have a reference group, a support group, they would have to come from across the country, and the men wouldn't like that."[25]

McLaughlin was a feminist, but she avoided a public focus on "women's issues." (This is a loaded term, and unpopular in many quarters.) She spoke with militant conviction about violence, discrimination and reproductive choice at women's rallies, but in the Commons she emphasized her concern for working families, the unemployed and the poor. Her support for aboriginal causes brought her to a contradiction with feminism; her support for aboriginal self-government was absolute, despite the fears of some women about the extreme male bias of some aboriginal councils.

In three months from April 1990 through June 1990, McLaughlin raised 60 questions in the House;[26] 5 or 6 might be described as dealing with women's issues. In another sample period, March and April 1991, none of McLaughlin's 17 questions were specifically directed at women.

McLaughlin tried to give all her work a feminist tinge, though, with what she and her advisers called "new politics."

Audrey was very, very strong on articulating what she called "the new politics." One element of that was that you don't yell and scream about everything that happens and you don't always go for the one-liner. You pick your issues, you're thoughtful about them ... So rather than having Audrey out every day on every issue, like Sheila Copps being as crazy as possible to get a clip, we decided to do it slower and more deliberately.[27]

This was to be a kinder, gentler politics, a less partisan politics. McLaughlin showed a strong interest in policy, but she tried to point up the human side of issues, the effects on children or the poor. She would talk with reporters about the need to involve the Opposition in government decisions, and ask whether the public had been consulted. In some ways — and this is a comparison McLaughlin made herself — she had a lot in common with the very un-feminist Preston Manning, except that she failed.

The key to Manning's success and McLaughlin's lack of it, says Michael Balagus, was consistency. Manning had absolute authority within his party, which gave him the luxury of sticking to a message he liked month after month. McLaughlin, says Balagus, constantly had to defend caucus and provincial government positions she disagreed with. She also felt pressure from New Democrats who wanted her to compete with Jean Chrétien on every issue, and from those who wanted a more "bombastic, rattle-the-walls" style.[28] This suggests a dilemma for party politics: that the only way to remain totally honest and speak from the heart, as voters would like, is to run a dictatorship like Preston Manning or Ross Perot. Ed Broadbent claimed this freedom sometimes — for example, when he spoke on the Constitution — but the NDP would not press it on McLaughlin, and she did not claim it.

When she toured, the media in the regions gave McLaughlin the attention due a visiting celebrity. The media in Parliament kept an eye on her, but they did not grant her high status. Perhaps, as a study from the Royal Commission on Electoral Reform suggests, any woman leader would have been at a disadvantage before the Press Gallery. It says the media view that the NDP chose McLaughlin because she was a woman — a view echoed in this chapter — represents a tendency among reproters and editors to "subtly put down women politicians." The study says reporters focus on women's looks and hair in a way they would never do for men, they neglect past accomplishments, they demand that women politicians take responsibility for the actions of all other women, and they use the term "feminist" as a negative personal characteristic rather than as a reference to a broad and varied set of political outlooks.[29]

The men of the Sun newspaper chain clearly loathed McLaughlin. Canadian Press reporters in Ottawa tell of a CP editor in Toronto who tried to sabotage McLaughlin's first day on the job by assigning a story about how a woman leader was bound to fail. The assignment was overruled by a senior woman editor.

Political columnist Jane Taber of *The Ottawa Citizen* says male reporters are "intimidated by strong women" and disliked McLaughlin. But Taber also faults McLaughlin for her one-dimensional public persona. "She has so much trouble talking about her personal life that people couldn't get a fix on who she was."[30]

Denise Harrington from CBC television says the Hill media were open to the presence of women leaders, especially with the rise of Sheila Copps and Kim Campbell. McLaughlin and her team, she says, suffered from the same disadvantage faced by any third party. "They were competing with a bigger opposition party that was higher in the polls. To steal attention away from the Liberals, they would have needed an edge, but it just didn't happen. They rarely added anything new. And there was a lot of sharing of questions with other NDP MPs, obviously a deliberate decision on her part."[31]

Geoffrey York of *The Globe and Mail*, who wrote several major articles on the NDP, says McLaughlin simply failed to learn the basics of her trade. He says Gallery reporters judge politicians by "how many jabs they get in at the prime minister during Question Period," not by their comments about caucuses working as a team. In this context, he says, McLaughlin could never capture the 20-second clip as well as a more practised MP like Dave Barrett. "She's not perceived as a strong leader, and I don't think she is a strong leader. She had trouble articulating why the NDP was different, or why people should vote for the NDP in the 90s."[32]

As the months went by, McLaughlin's speeches and her performance with the media improved in every detail. However, she rarely made the crucial final step of addressing the issues in both a distinctive and confident way. Most readers and viewers saw only a fleeting image of an ineffectual leader. The party, in fact, became convinced that her handlers were keeping her from public view. Preston Manning had more luck; besides having a male identity (imagine Manning as a woman), he won the ideological sympathy of media managers with his anti-deficit, anti-politician, anti-government message. If Audrey McLaughlin was like Pierre Trudeau in coming to politics in middle life, she also resembled him in her aloof and sometimes cranky personality. She was not the ideal vehicle for the new politics. Trudeau employed veteran fixers to keep his fences mended, charming socializers like Jim Coutts and Senator Keith Davey. Allan Blakeney, the mandarin-turned-premier in Saskatchewan, counted on Bill Knight, a genial hayseed who knew every New Democrat's name, when they were born, and whom they hated. McLaughlin needed to hire a fence-mender or two. Instead, she chose Les Campbell and Michael Balagus, image-builders, young men who could focus on her needs, cool and aloof from the outside world. The signal went out to hundreds of active party members: the new woman leader was replacing the unpopular "boys in the back room" with more boys.

Considering that her chief of staff supervised 35 people, one might have expected McLaughlin to hire a manager. However, she placed a higher priority on finding someone who knew the NDP. Several of her women supporters qualified. Unfortunately, according to interim chief of staff John Walsh, none were available. Ginny Devine was married and tied to Winnipeg; Sharon Vance was married in Montreal; Carol Phillips was married in Toronto.[33] McLaughlin settled on Campbell, a 29-year-old man from Winnipeg who had worked with the Howard Pawley NDP government and then with the Manitoba NDP opposition under Gary Doer.

McLaughlin and Campbell agreed to hire a communications director and deputy chief of staff. Many expected them to choose a woman who could work in both official languages. Instead, McLaughlin went with Campbell's choice of his brother-in-law, 34-year-old Michael Balagus, a former Manitoba NDP speechwriter.

One by one, Broadbent's assistants left. McLaughlin's new policy assistant was a male Westerner; her new speechwriter was a male Westerner. This struck many of us on the Hill as odd; when I made a list in summer 1990, I found that McLaughlin had fewer women on staff than Broadbent had. The only senior woman, research director Arlene Wortsman, was a holdover from the Broadbent period.

Campbell had remarkable presence for a person of his age. He radiated calm and confidence, and remained unshakeable in a crisis. Balagus, intense and more of a joker, also stayed calm under pressure. Together they helped McLaughlin through her speeches, her negotiations with the provincial NDP barons and her media appearances. Their chief task was to give life to the new politics. They agreed with their boss on the need for a direct approach: the leader should look for opportunities to say what she meant and speak from the heart. They held this view until the day they were forced out, believing that despite McLaughlin's lack of polish, and perhaps because of it, she remained the NDP's strongest card.

However, the strategists' view of the finer points of the new politics was far from innocent. It was shaped by what they read in *Campaigns and Elections* magazine and heard from the party's contacts in Washington. In the new U.S. politics, the politician was required to escape the Capitol and be seen among the people. When I moved from constitutional memo-writing to caucus flyer-writing, Balagus assigned me to write a leaflet on McLaughlin's new style of leadership. He and Campbell were keen on a television ad for a U.S. re-election campaign. Instead of shots of Congress, the ad showed a veteran senator from Texas arranging funding for a rural school-bus service. Excited by this approach, the strategists asked me to find a similar story about McLaughlin in the Yukon. Unhappily, her Yukon assistants told me, there was none.

Campaigns and Elections also advised the new politician to by-pass reporters and reach the public through media vehicles like fireside chats and televised town halls. Accordingly, Balagus and Campbell persuaded McLaughlin to write a book about herself. *A Woman's Place*, published in autumn 1992, sums up the life and views of an ordinary — perhaps distressingly ordinary — Canadian woman. It is remarkably light on achievement. McLaughlin writes of meetings with Mohawks and ambassadors, but except for the notes on two pressure campaigns she ran as a backbench MP, the book offers voters no evidence that McLaughlin could resolve disagreements or bring about change in the real world.[34]

As McLaughlin's term wore on, many in the party were also looking for evidence. Could she even manage her own advisers? Campbell and Balagus were bright and hard-working. They understood the leader's ideas about the new politics, and they sympathized with McLaughlin's feminist convictions. But they were also political hardball players of the old school, intent on hoarding information and winning control. Their actions over the course of many months raised questions about whether McLaughlin herself believed in her

agenda for change — starting in the MPs' offices and the party
headquarters, and moving in ripples from there.

The brothers-in-law had a clumsy, seat-of-the-pants style of staff
relations that put them in violation of the new politics almost every
day. Their occasional briefing sessions for Parliament Hill assistants
came straight from a military briefing tent, with pointers, mono-
logues, and "any questions?" Their offhand hiring decisions provoked a stream of formal grievances. The Hill represented a central
reserve of NDP organizers and a storehouse of brainpower. Like the
caucus, the leader's office squandered these crucial resources.

Soon after he brought Balagus on board, Campbell began to take
on tasks that had previously been handled at the federal headquarters.
He already had first rights to polling information, since his good
friend, David Gotthilf, had been hired as the party's pollster. In
addition to this, he and Balagus took charge of advertising and related
campaign work. Yard by yard, federal secretary Dick Proctor lost a
quiet struggle with the brothers-in-law. When he resigned, he did not
go in fury — his wife had moved to a senior government job in
Regina — but he left without regrets. He resurfaced as the federal
campaign planner for Saskatchewan, and helped save five of the
party's nine seats in 1993.

> I don't know who was supposed to resolve it. It seems to me
> that in every election the party has ever run, the party and not
> the leader's office ran the campaign. In this instance, once
> Balagus got into place, there was a deliberate effort by him and
> Les to assume as much responsibility as they possibly could.
> They wanted control over polling and strategic planning, and
> to suck resources out of Somerset Street [the federal headquar-
> ters].
>
> I think Audrey has to wear some of that. It was a glaring
> mistake to hire people who were related to each other and put
> them in such senior capacities, because it always seemed to me
> it was a two-against-one proposition: even in those rare in-
> stances where I thought I was winning, they could always go
> back to the Leader and turn the tables. I just think it exhibited
> bad management on her part.
>
> Les and Michael acquired a reputation from one end of the
> country to the other, and not a positive reputation.[35]

By 1991, Campbell was well established as McLaughlin's right arm. He helped her to draft affirmative action guidelines to be approved at the summer convention in Halifax. The guidelines imposed an obligation on every local NDP association to seek out possible "affirmative action" candiates — that is, women or members of minorities. There was back-room resistance to what Dawn Black calls a "monumental change," mostly from older male MPs, but the convention adopted the guidelines without public dissent.[36] The resistance softened over time, and the NDP became the first Canadian party ever to nominate 100 women for a federal election.

At the same convention, McLaughlin and Campbell worked together to achieve a compromise on the Constitution. McLaughlin, as chair of a Constitution committee of NDP leaders, had bounced a draft resolution around the provincial leaders' offices and major labour headquarters. The draft underwent surgery at Halifax, as Bob Rae and Manitoba's Gary Doer took turns undoing each other's work. Out on the convention floor, delegates spent an hour in workshops on the Constitution. When the workshops had reported, the prearranged resolution was produced and voted on. The process was tidy, it was quick, and it produced a resolution with no rough edges. In fact, said one party staff member, the whole thing was brokered more brazenly than anything ever tried by Broadbent.

For some of the optimists who had supported McLaughlin in 1989, it was a cruel moment of disillusionment. "I don't think fraud is too strong a word," says a former party youth leader. "If this was the yardstick to be used to measure the progress of the new politics in the NDP, it was a pretty stubby yardstick."

For Marion Dewar, the unfolding of events in McLaughlin's office brought back nostalgia for the first moment of victory. "It was so exciting. We thought there would be a whole new debate in the party. We would be doing things differently. Our Question Period had always been taken from *The Globe and Mail* front page, so we never talked about what needed talking about. Audrey and I used to discuss that. I thought we'd have women's issues in there a lot more. I talked to Audrey and to Michael and to Les about the needs of children, the environment, the future. They told me they didn't want her to become a single-issue candidate. Instead, we went back to *The Globe and Mail*, we went back to business as usual."[37]

Neither McLaughlin's friends nor her female assistants can explain how a feminist leader came to depend so completely on two male strategists. Historian Alan Whitehorn calls it ironic that they wielded such "extraordinary power" in McLaughlin's office.[38] As this power grew, the strategists behaved more and more as if they and McLaughlin were surrounded by adversaries — not only in the other parties and the media, but also in the parliamentary caucus, among the MPs whose job it was to put the NDP's program into action.

4

A Caucus Adrift

*The New Democratic Party does not have a natural pool of compe-
tent managers. This destroys its ability to do things. The machine is
too complicated. The energies flowing up from below are lost inside.
If this is not corrected, the party will never get results, whatever the
quality of the democracy or the ideas.*

— Michel Agnaieff[1]

Perhaps the worst night of Audrey McLaughlin's leadership came on
Wednesday, February 26, 1992, when enraged NDP members of
Parliament denounced her, one after another, for questioning their
pension plan.

The deluxe MPs' pension, payable immediately after six years'
service, had become a favourite target of talk-show hosts, business
lobbies and anyone who wanted to trash politicians. Speaking to the
Commons on Monday morning, McLaughlin had proposed a few
common-sense changes to the plan. The age of eligibility for pensions should be set at a standard public-sector level, and nobody who
worked for the federal government should draw an MPs' pension.

News reports of McLaughlin's speech triggered a wave of enthu-
siastic phone calls and faxes from the public. But senior NDP MPs
demanded a formal session for Wednesday night, all staff excluded,
where they rained fire on her head.

In their eyes, McLaughlin and Les Campbell had ambushed them.
She had betrayed them. Her proposals threatened their children's
future. "If you want a fight, you'll get one!" roared one champion of
the downtrodden. An Ontario veteran wept, and said no employer
would ever hire a socialist ex-MP. Others sat astonished; nobody,
however, spoke in the leader's defence. "Audrey had the vision to
speak out, but they shit on her," says Phil Edmonston, who was a
Montreal-area MP. "When it came to their own dough, forget about
principles."[2]

McLaughlin returned to her Centre Block office in tears. "It was a turning point, and I knew it at the time," says Les Campbell, the leader's principal secretary. "That's when I knew the caucus either hated her or were indifferent. Even her supporters weren't very effective."[3]

For years, the MPs had fielded letters from voters asking about their pension plan and its $140 million (and growing) unfunded liability. McLaughlin had named two caucus committees in succession to work out a response to such inquiries, but they had never reported.

When the government passed the word that it wanted changes to public-sector pensions in general, Campbell saw an opportunity to raise questions about MPs' pensions. He asked sympathetic MPs to attend the regular Monday morning strategy session, and at that meeting they agreed that McLaughlin should go ahead. Other MPs complained that they had been left in the dark, and never would have agreed to the content of McLaughlin's short speech.

> I remind members of this house there is no other Canadian who receives a pension after six years.
> The autoworkers, whose plant shut down just today, certainly will not have that kind of pension. The fish plant workers who saw their jobs disappear last week will not have that kind of pension.[4]

Once upon a time, Stanley Knowles had scored political points by opposing pay raises for MPs. But this group of MPs, say caucus observers, felt great affection for their pensions, and didn't like McLaughlin playing with their money. They would need that money, too. They had the feeling they were on a sinking ship, and part of it was her fault.

"They say that every NDP convention has a revolt on one topic or another," says former MP John Brewin. "It might be smoking, or whatever. This issue allowed a catharsis along the divisions that had been there all along ... The fault line was quite simple: between those who had been elected in 1988 [about half the caucus, with no claim to a pension], and virtually everybody else."[5] In the end, after venting their feelings, the MPs agreed to stand by McLaughlin's remarks for official purposes, but they refused to fuel further public anger against pensions. There would be no more speeches, and no effort to distribute McLaughlin's speech, even to party members.

The fatal flaws in the NDP's parliamentary wing had caught up with it once again. The MPs, having engineered a state of disorganization in the caucus, failed to act on an important problem; the leader took unilateral action; the MPs reacted and then forgot the issue, without addressing the underlying problems. On the issue itself, they proved themselves to be out of tune with a public mood that was ready to rise up and destroy them.

The parliamentary caucus functions as the centre of power in a decentralized party. The Federal Council meets twice a year; when Parliament sits, caucus gathers every day to review the issues and set the party line. Caucus members work day after day to explain the NDP perspective and to influence politicians from other parties, lobby groups, and the media.

The MPs are ambassadors for the party, but are not, in most respects, responsible to the party organization. They are united in spirit on most points of principle, but they spend their individual office budgets as they wish, and in making their spending decisions they pursue individual political priorities. Critics complain that New Democrats can't run a pop stand; on the matter of caucus, most NDP MPs don't even see that there is a pop stand to be run. Where a social agency or a business might choose three or four practical objectives, members of the New Democrat caucus chase a hundred. Over many years, they have built an institution without corporate identity or corporate discipline. The caucus executive lacks the authority to organize MPs' resources in a rational way, even when the party's survival is at risk.

Within this framework, the leader of the perpetual third party in Parliament has limited power to dominate her fellow MPs, even if she wanted to. Unlike the prime minister or the prime-minister-in-waiting, she has no cabinet posts to entice MPs with, no jobs with federal agencies. She has only moral suasion and whatever favours or junkets the Whip and House Leader might control.

All federal NDP leaders have faced some trials.[6] Tommy Douglas had colleagues who leaked caucus decisions to the media, and his caucus split over the War Measures Act. David Lewis, a leader with a will of steel, ran up against a hard-bitten faction who liked to defeat his proposals "just for fun."[7] Half a dozen of Ed Broadbent's colleagues fought him in public on the Constitution issue. However, as a leader sworn to a system of leadership among equals, and a relative newcomer to Parliament, the Member for the Yukon faced special problems.

Politics tends to attract competitive, driven people. The New Democrat MPs owed their seats to their strength of purpose, and each was a local celebrity. Jim Fulton had taken his truck over every road in northwestern B.C. to win four straight elections. Dan Heap, with three election wins, maintained a formidable coalition of multicultural activists, artists, students and trade unionists in downtown Toronto. John Rodriguez won twice, lost twice, and then won two more in the Nickel Belt around Sudbury. Most of the MPs believed they had political insight that no leader or pollster could match.

As elected officials representing 100,000 people each, many Canadian MPs experience extreme stress and fatigue, to the point where they may become chronically moody and unpredictable. For this, they earn the wage of a suburban school vice-principal. They can also claim tax-free expense payments in order to rent an apartment in Ottawa and keep some suits in the closet. Too much, say the editorials and the talk-show callers, too much; the MPs should work harder in Ottawa, harder in their ridings, and cut their own pay.

Most New Democrat MPs live apart from their families. They spend three weekends a month in mid-air, and do countless favours for people regardless of political stripe. Small eruptions at home clamour for their attention: a change in postal delivery times, a grant for a seniors' centre, a blocked culvert under some federal railway tracks. Their assistants reunite immigrant families, track down lost pension cheques, and help Janie write her essay for school; they also do small political tasks such as making certificates for high school grads or fridge calendars bearing the MP's photo. Out of four or five staff, one assistant often keeps track of a cabinet portfolio such as energy or transport, and helps draft that tough question to the minister for inclusion in the householder report.

Members of McLaughlin's first caucus travelled to remote corners of Canada to address union meetings and citizens' groups. They kept close watch on their provincial parties and took care not to differ with provincial leaders. They attended parliamentary committees and plugged away for amendments to bills. They buttonholed ministers to plead their cases. Joy Langan won more research on breast cancer and a ban on artificial breast implants. Svend Robinson persuaded the government to concede the principle of non-discrimination against gays in the armed forces. Jim Karpoff talked the Minister of Revenue into imposing a tobacco export tax; the tax cut sales to

U.S.-based smugglers so effectively that the tobacco industry rose up and forced the government to withdraw it. But this backbenchers' lobbying of government, such a key part of the American congressional system, had no formal or public status in the NDP: as with so much caucus activity, there was no training for MPs and no analysis of the possibilities.

Until October 1993, the NDP caucus received about $9 million per year from the House of Commons for staff salaries and office expenses. Three-quarters of that was parcelled out by the House directly to MPs. The remainder, controlled by McLaughlin, paid for central research and communications units that provided support for both the leader and individual MPs, with most staff officers assigned to an issue area.

Altogether, about 240 people worked for the NDP on the Hill or in community offices. Perhaps 50, some with master's degrees, kept office budgets and answered the phone; half a dozen worked as economic researchers. A hundred or more helped citizens fill out UI claims and built 50 sets of mailing lists; half a dozen might be available to work part-time on urgent public awareness campaigns. MP Chris Axworthy had done some work with Roy Romanow's Saskatchewan provincial caucus, which he described as a tight ship. The federal caucus, he said, "wasn't a ship at all, just a bunch of little rafts, or the wreckage of a ship."[8]

Soon after McLaughlin took over as leader, the caucus moved its weekly meetings from a sunny boardroom in the West Block to a concrete-walled chamber under the Peace Tower. The MPs sat at tables arranged in a square, usually joined by the party secretary and either the Canadian Labour Congress president or the CLC's political officer, Pat Kerwin. A translator perched in a booth nearby, talking to herself. At the end of the room away from the leader, a few visitors and a gaggle of staff occupied some rows of chairs.

The meetings were long. McLaughlin worked to deliver consensus leadership. She wanted to draw all players on-side, to give everyone a stake in the outcome, and thereby to reach the best and most durable decisions. She says her job was to "raise their comfort level"[9] with difficult decisions. "Audrey genuinely wanted people to come forward with ideas on where we should be going," says former MP Dawn Black. "But there were some people who didn't think it was real."[10]

For most MPs, on most days, her style allowed them the freedom they desired. As party spokespeople on issues such as justice or immigration, they developed their own arguments and looked for publicity for themselves. On non-urgent questions — for example, MPs' pensions — they could use the consensus principle as an excuse to delay and duck. On high-pressure issues driven by the government, the caucus usually worked through its differences to the point where it could vote as a group.

When an MP took a public stand that embarrassed the others, as Phil Edmonston did periodically on Quebec, the group made an earnest effort to win a promise of future good behaviour. McLaughlin disciplined MPs only twice — once after a public split on the government's constitutional referendum bill, and once when finance critic Steven Langdon called the NDP premier of Ontario to account.

Underneath the relative harmony, however, many MPs sensed a background of discontent. It never decayed into the factional bloodletting that plagued the Tories for so many years; it was more a mumbling in the corridors, a sullen questioning of where the party was headed. The opposition to McLaughlin could not be traced to Dave Barrett, who was always lavish in his expressions of loyalty at caucus meetings, but it was clearly centred in the more conservative Western MPs. When consensus broke down and caucus had to vote, says Chris Axworthy, the leader generally scraped through by just three or four votes. Joy Langan says the rules for this conflict never became clear.

> There were only 5 women MPs, and 39 men, and I was really quite surprised at how even some of the younger members could never come to grips with the fact that there was a woman running the show. Whether that was personality, whether they thought Dave Barrett would have done a better job, or whether Barrett just became a symbol to use, I don't know ...
>
> I saw the caucus test Broadbent from time to time, but with Audrey it was constant. There was constantly another agenda going on behind the scenes. Those people with the other agenda didn't talk to the women MPs, because they thought we were the first line of defence for the boss, I guess ... There was a constant sense that the cauldron was almost to the boil.

Some who watched the caucus, men and women, deny that McLaughlin suffered because of her gender, but they equate her "consensus" style with a failure to set direction. McLaughlin and her senior staff, by this account, lacked the talent or the taste for placating opponents, reining in over-eager allies, or keeping debate focused.

Broadbent never asked for a decision that hadn't been brokered. Dissidents always knew the meeting was stacked against them. Audrey never learned the value of solidifying her support before a meeting. She'd be surprised when people spoke against her. On the other hand, it didn't happen that often, because she was committed to so few positions. When it came to the test, with MPs' pensions or the referendum, there was a lot of tension because nobody knew which way things were going.[11]

Many MPs complained that McLaughlin's senior aides built a barrier around her. Les Campbell and Michael Balagus were unlikely deputies for a feminist politician — young, arrogant and trained in the hierarchy of a Manitoba NDP government. Too often, their idea of reaching out was to take an MP to the woodshed. Balagus admits he came to his job with the wrong attitude.

I had never worked in opposition politics. The last job I had was working for the premier of Manitoba. If he had a problem, he would tell me to go down to talk to Minister X. You did that, and they listened. If you were on the premier's staff, you walked in with a certain amount of authority. I just assumed in my naïveté that the same thing would happen in Ottawa. By the time I learned my lesson, I had probably done irreparable damage.[12]

Soon after he arrived in Ottawa, Les Campbell aggressively confronted Lorne Nystrom about some of his comments to the media. Nystrom had been granting interviews as an MP since Campbell was in Sunday school, and the two got into a furious row over Nystrom's habit of taking non-partisan positions on the Constitution. As a result, McLaughlin permanently lost a channel to a senior MP.

Campbell now says he mishandled relations with MPs, and this damaged the links between McLaughlin and the natural leaders in caucus. The small caucus executive could have helped set a corporate direction, but Campbell did not see it at the time.

That was a tremendous failing of mine. I saw those executive jobs as shit jobs, as a major joke ... Audrey was preoccupied with herself, she was withdrawn. On a staff level, there was nobody who cared or thought what the executive were doing was important. In the caucus, there were so many agendas, and no place for collective action ... The MPs who were trying had no place to turn.[13]

The brothers-in-law held court in Campbell's office, directly across from McLaughlin's in the Centre Block. MPs' assistants who dropped in were treated to a fund of anecdotes on the stupidity of caucus members. One assistant says they labelled each MP as "pro-Audrey and anti-Audrey. The anti-Audrey people, they thought, would never change, and the pro-Audrey people could be taken for granted." When another aide met with Campbell over a problem Dave Barrett was having with the media, Campbell surprised him by charging that "Barrett keeps trying to do Audrey in."[14]

This attitude caused resentment. Anonymous MPs grumbled to *The Toronto Star* about McLaughlin's leadership. In response, Balagus told the paper that some MPs had never accepted her leadership, "a small group — but a powerful group — who are holding us back."[15] A few weeks later Campbell expressed public relief that with the summer recess, MPs were no longer in Ottawa to "plot and panic."[16]

Chris Axworthy says his colleagues viewed Campbell and Balagus as incompetent, although he also understands the strategists' impatience with caucus. The MPs discussed ways of putting the brothers-in-law to the sword, but somehow the issue never surfaced on the caucus agenda. "We were a bunch of chickens. We never did want to confront any of these difficult problems, ... so for three years things just trundled along as we went from 41 per cent down to 6 or 7 ... Plus, we didn't know who to replace them with."[17] Instead of taking collective action, MPs went one by one to urge McLaughlin to fire her advisers. She took this pressure as a test of her leadership, says her long-time ally Marion Dewar. "She said, 'You attack them, you're attacking me. They're the only people I can trust.' "[18]

As for McLaughlin's direct relationship with the MPs, accounts vary widely. She kept close ties with the four other women in caucus. The men, despite Campbell's belief that many hated her, seem to have maintained a personal respect tinged with sympathy. However, there was also increasing frustration, even among her convention supporters. "Audrey made a mistake in the selection of her key people," says John Brewin. "That's forgivable — everybody makes mistakes — but then she never changed them ... More important, though, she never developed a sense of where she wanted to take the party."[19]

Sandra Mitchell, who eventually replaced Campbell as principal secretary, was shocked to discover McLaughlin's distance from other New Democrats on the Hill. Mitchell says McLaughlin refused to consider any special program of fence-mending meetings or visits with MPs; any MP who had a problem, McLaughlin said, could come and see her.[20] Campbell's final memo to his boss may shed light on their shared outlook. In it, he identified a tendency in caucus to resist disciplined effort and grope blindly for salvation.

> It is important to take people's ideas seriously but it is just as important not to be sidetracked every time another good idea comes by. I've had weeks where I felt like a yoyo because I chased three or four of Nelson's great ideas only to remember too late that they weren't leading anywhere ...
>
> Every task can be prioritized according to who it is important to and for. I continue to believe the order is this — Leader, Party officials (Julie, Nancy, etc.), Party and Union activists and Leaders (Bob White, Carol Phillips, Ray Martin, Michael Lewis, Marion Dewar, etc.), Caucus members, Leader's staff, Hill staff. The problem with this prioritization is that the caucus and Hill staff get upset but in the end, they do have their own resources and their own constituencies within the party and the country and will survive ...
>
> Having said this, it is very important to spend some time with the caucus in the next month or two, especially on incumbent election readiness, and to improve staff morale a bit. But, as usual, everyone's morale will be fine when we rise in the polls.[21]

The 44 members of the NDP caucus were divided by personal priorities and ambitions, and hindered by disorganization. Nonetheless, they remained united in spirit by common experience and a sense of mission. The New Democrat MPs were the holdouts against the New World Order. They were Parliament's do-gooders, the butt of scorn from the right-wing media. They were labour organizers, storefront lawyers, lifelong agitators; McLaughlin was one of at least five social workers.

In the House of Commons, they usually stood together.

In January 1991, the United States launched the bombing of Baghdad in retaliation for Iraq's invasion of Kuwait. The Conservatives supported the American action and committed Canadian troops to the offensive. The NDP opposed the government's decision, risking public hostility. An estimated 75 per cent of Canadians supported the Pentagon's strike against Saddam Hussein. The Liberals flip-flopped to go along with popular feeling, and some in the NDP caucus wanted to do the same.

McLaughlin called repeated caucus meetings, three or four times a day, until everyone had accepted a common strategy. McLaughlin and acting external affairs critic John Brewin hoped to give MPs "some running room" by supporting Canada's military role in enforcing sanctions against Iraq,[22] but McLaughlin delivered two strongly anti-war speeches. For some, they recalled the NDP's opposition to the War Measures Act in 1970.

> If we go to war now, we will be haunted by each and every casualty. We will wonder if we had tried to wait for other options and if we had taken a pro-active approach to peace and not a reactive approach to war if that would have made a real difference.
>
> This dreadful war will cost us far too much. Worse, a victory will be no guarantee of peace in this part of the world. The defeat of Saddam Hussein in Iraq may make it even harder to achieve our objective: peace and security in the Middle East.[23]

Michael Balagus remembers McLaughlin's Gulf War speeches as pure "new politics," the best ever — distinctive, principled, from the heart, and excellent television to boot. Nelson Riis says other MPs would have done it differently, but they decided to give McLaughlin "the benefit of the doubt" in her handling of a complicated issue.

> I'm not to this day certain about what our position on the Gulf War was. I know what people think it was, and I guess that's what Audrey intended. I think we decided to support the Gulf War, but not with up-front combat troops. The perception was that we were against participating.[24]

The NDP managed a similar show of unity on other emotional issues. On abortion, New Democrat conventions had set out a clear pro-choice position for MPs to follow. Even so, several were inclined to vote for Justice Minister Kim Campbell's proposed restrictions. Joy Langan and Dawn Black spent several days visiting MPs in their offices and talking them through their doubts. In the end, even Catholic school principal Steve Butland voted against the Campbell package.

On difficult economic issues, the caucus maintained unity in Parliament despite public indifference or hostility. On free trade with the United States, the NDP supported abrogation. On the Goods and Services Tax, the NDP called for abolition.

However, in working together to make these views known outside Parliament, the New Democrats were less successful.

Caucus meetings produced no written reports to staff. Besides trade and the GST, the caucus agreed at various meetings to run public awareness campaigns on the environment, VIA Rail, all federal budgets, postal service, unemployment insurance, the government's Green Plan, parliamentary reform, fair taxes, NAFTA, the Constitution, the referendum law, drug prices, the constitutional referendum, job creation, the NDP Jobs Plan and Senate abolition. What did such an agreement mean? It meant that 2, or 6, or 10 MPs had a licence to use Issue X as a way to win political benefits. News of the decision would float down to somebody's assistant; he or she then snared a few colleagues into a little work club, in the absence of either deadlines or stated objectives.

All these public campaigns, considering the potential of the $9 million machine, were tiny in scope. The fragmentation of caucus effort, combined with nervousness about whether NDP proposals were in fact practical, prevented the MPs from committing real resources. The caucus could have worked more effectively to find better alternatives, share their findings, and help to co-ordinate action across the communities of the Canadian left.

Throughout 1989 and 1990, the caucus ran a low-level campaign against the Goods and Services Tax. Rob Sutherland, who worked in the six-member Caucus Resources Office, spent weeks assembling a mailing list of New Democrat supporters. He designed buttons, wrote some anti-GST literature and organizing tips, and prodded MPs' staff to help him mail thousands of kits. None of this was concerted with the Action Canada Network's anti-GST campaign; ACN campaign co-ordinator Murray Dobbin recalls a "total disconnection between the NDP and the real world." When Dobbin asked to see the NDP's tax alternatives in the summer of 1990, he says the party had nothing on hand. There might be a document ready by February, he was told — that is, after the scheduled introduction of the tax.

In mid-1992, with labour and the Action Canada Network pushing the party to make some noise about trade, a few caucus members agreed to join an anti-NAFTA campaign. Trade critic Dave Barrett was a star orator, but never an organizer, and so Manitoba MP Rod Murphy offered his part-time services and those of his assistant, Guy Freedman, to Barrett. They circulated several issues of an anti-NAFTA newsletter to labour, ACN groups, and across labour's Solinet computer network. Two MPs visited Washington to meet with anti-NAFTA members of Congress, drawing some national media coverage. MPs' staff tipped off regional anti-NAFTA activists on the government's restriction of the parliamentary trade commit-tee's right to travel, leading to some local protests and more news coverage.

Even this ad hoc, part-time effort won extensive media publicity. Would a more disciplined campaign against NAFTA have made the issue a winner for the NDP? Some have argued that the party lacked well-researched alternatives, and the MPs would have been wasting their time. Why not find the alternatives, or else admit honestly that there were none? Some in the NDP also complain that the party lacked effective allies, that the Action Canada Network leaders spent all their time down the hall lobbying the Liberals. Barrett and McLaughlin pleaded with Action Canada's Tony Clarke to forget the Liberals and get behind the NDP. But again, was the Action Canada strategy a cause of the NDP's failure on the trade deal, or a result of the NDP's long record as a weak and disorganized ally?

"We believed in this issue," says former aide Guy Freedman about the handful of New Democrats on the Hill who joined in. "We were all doing it out of the goodness of our heart. Nobody else was going to do it, so we did it. That's no way to run a steamship."[25]

While the anti-NAFTA campaign puttered along, McLaughlin released the NDP Jobs Plan. The Plan had been tagged as the party's election platform document, and MPs' offices mailed out thousands of copies. However, the caucus promotion of the Plan at the grass roots followed the usual pattern. Phrases and fragments would pop up in leaflets, householder reports and speeches, but there was no body within the caucus with the authority to co-ordinate, set objec-tives or evaluate results.

One strategist who served in various mini-campaigns grew weary of watching them roll out of the chute. "There was little to no caucus commitment over the long haul. If something didn't work in a month, it would be dropped after the next poll ... There was no sense of entering any campaign beyond doing some mailings."

Brian Gardiner, a young MP who had once worked as a caucus assistant, also got discouraged.

> Whenever the suggestion was made that we launch a campaign or extend it beyond questions in the House, it never happened. It always got ground to a halt. I don't know why. It was said about issues like the GST and NAFTA and free trade that we weren't credible, so why do anything? I gave up, and started preparing my own information kits on our alternatives to the GST ...
>
> The final vote on NAFTA, we all marched into the House at the same time. That was thought to be a really unique and new idea.[26]

The NDP caucus's allergy to planning and management was remarkable in a party dedicated to proving the efficiency of the public sector. As caucus chair before she became leader, McLaughlin had hired Marc Eliesen, a one-time caucus research director and soon-to-be chair of Ontario Hydro, to come in and suggest changes to the caucus structure. Eliesen had pointed diplomatically to the gross waste of effort involved in running 44 separate shops, but nothing had happened. Either the MPs liked their independence too much, or they were blind to the benefits of working together. To change anything, says John Brewin, McLaughlin would have had to act in her first six months as leader. "An experienced principal secretary who was determined might have done something ... Support for it would have to be fought and won."[27]

The NDP MPs and their staff paddled hard on their little rafts. The harder they paddled, the lower the party sank in public esteem. The New Democrats mailed out flyers linking Conservative policies with unemployment and poverty, and yet found themselves falling behind the Tories. They howled at the Liberals to take a clear stand on taxes, trade or spending; meanwhile, the Liberals rose in the polls. In the West, the small-town media hammered away on a Reform Party agenda resurrected from the 1920s: recall, referendum, death to partisan politics.

The New Democrats could sense hostility to all politicians in the conversations along Main Street. They knew they worked hard to serve the public and they hoped the mood would pass. Blame it on Mulroney, they told each other; he makes us all look like bums. When the NDP's chance came to join the populist anti-politician wave and attack MPs' pensions, the caucus declined. For some MPs, the world of "Us and Them" had become inverted. "Us" had become the hard-working elected official, snatching a few parliamentary meals in the course of a busy week; "Them" was a mob of ungrateful voters.

In the fall of 1992, the NDP suffered through the wrenching ordeal of the constitutional referendum. Thousands of party members voted against their own New Democrat MPs; local NDP executives and labour councils split in half. On a Monday morning after it was over, with the NDP on the Hill still in shock, McLaughlin called her staff together to announce Les Campbell's resignation. Her remarks were brief. She emphasized that she had not fired him and that he had remained a professional to the end. There were no questions. Balagus's explanation to me, later in the day, was that his brother-in-law was burnt out by the referendum and tired of fighting with MPs and other critics in the party.

McLaughlin, always isolated, had lost a pillar of personal support. Sandra Mitchell, a Saskatoon lawyer and former federal party president, offered her services as principal secretary, and McLaughlin accepted. Mitchell arrived in Ottawa after Christmas. For two weeks she made a diligent effort to meet with caucus and staff and prepare a first report. On a Saturday afternoon she met with McLaughlin in the sparsely furnished living room of the leader's Ottawa apartment.

Mitchell drew a portrait of a caucus and a party in crisis. Above all, she blamed Campbell and Balagus. "Leaders are very ordinary people. Where they excel is in their ability to judge others. If they surround themselves with the brightest and the best they begin to look extraordinary."[28] She said the brothers-in-law had led McLaughlin down the wrong path and had botched the leader's relations with the caucus, the media and provincial sections. She said if McLaughlin did not pull up her socks, she would be remembered as a woman leader who knew nothing about leadership.

Mitchell's approach backfired. After three hours, McLaughlin rose, walked into her small kitchen, and said, "Well, I'm not going to fire Michael." It was their last consultation.[29]

As the federal party's standing fell below 10 per cent in the polls, the caucus entered the panic zone. The Steven Langdon episode brought its confusion into the open. Langdon, a former professor of economics, spoke out against Premier Rae's economic policies. The caucus overreacted, McLaughlin fired Langdon as finance critic, and the party erupted into an orgy of bickering and blame.

It was strange, perhaps, that Langdon should cause so much trouble. The Windsor-based MP was a popular veteran in the party and had finished a surprisingly strong third in the 1989 leadership race. During that campaign he had criticized McLaughlin for voting against the caucus position on the Meech Lake Accord; MPs should act like a team, he said, not like "a bunch of floating fish."[30] Later, when other MPs had complained about McLaughlin to *The Toronto Star*, Langdon had decried "a lack of discipline in caucus."[31] In general, he had seemed professional, though cool, in his dealings with McLaughlin.

By spring 1993, however, Langdon faced defeat in his riding. He blamed Bob Rae, and especially Rae's decision to reopen public-sector contracts. He lobbied members of the Rae cabinet without success. He knew that Audrey McLaughlin had visited Rae at Queen's Park and been rebuffed, as had senior labour leaders. Langdon's core of supporters in Windsor, starting with the Auto Workers, told him it was time to make his move if he wanted to save his political career.

At a caucus meeting on April 28, 1993, with McLaughlin absent, Langdon announced he would appear before reporters that day and release an open letter to Rae. The letter scolded the premier for an "unjustified preoccupation" with the deficit, for the phony social contract, and for cutting health care and other services. Speaking as the federal finance critic, he warned that drastic cuts to government spending would simply create more unemployment.

The other MPs asked Langdon to wait. They had planned a meeting with senior Ontario ministers for the next week. They wanted time to prepare a thoughtful, comprehensive statement on the Rae government's actions. Most of all, they did not want to face a public grilling, one by one, on why they did not speak out like Steven Langdon against the Rae government, the Romanow government or the Harcourt government.

Langdon listened, and walked out of the caucus room. A few minutes later he read his letter to reporters in the media room in the basement of the Centre Block. The caucus voted to approve a motion demanding that Langdon be dumped as finance critic. When McLaughlin returned to Ottawa that night, she agreed. With Balagus in Europe, and Sandra Mitchell estranged from her boss, this was McLaughlin's decision alone, and it turned Langdon's outburst into a national event.

Reporters canvassed MPs for their views. Riis and Nystrom supported the firing. Howard McCurdy, another former leadership contender, called the Langdon letter "a deliberate strategy to undermine the leader."[32] John Rodriguez from Sudbury agreed with Langdon that Rae's policies had hurt Ontario. Phil Edmonston issued a news release saying that Langdon spoke for many in the caucus. Nancy Riche, the president of the federal party, admitted that Langdon had consulted her on the contents of the letter, and said everything in it was "party policy."[33] CLC president Robert White suggested McLaughlin was trying to "put a blanket over" internal disagreement.[34] The issue was teamwork, McLaughlin insisted, not freedom of speech.

The controversy touched New Democrats in all regions. The switchboards were jammed at federal headquarters and on the Hill. Some party members, especially from Saskatchewan, attacked Langdon's disloyalty. Ray Martin, facing an impending election as Alberta leader, faxed McLaughlin the complaint that Langdon had probably cost him every seat in the province. Others tore into McLaughlin. Her long-time supporter Svend Robinson had joined a forest blockade against his own NDP government in British Columbia without paying any penalty in the federal caucus; in firing Langdon, McLaughlin was simply caving in to Bob Rae. Disillusioned Ontario party members, sometimes in tears, said Rae and McLaughlin were killing the NDP and the Ontario public service. This had gone beyond debate. There was rage in the party, a conviction that all sides in Ottawa were engaged in deceit and destruction.

Some media pundits echoed the view that Langdon's firing amounted to an attack on free speech, and tut-tutted over the NDP's hypocrisy. A few, more perceptive, linked the dispute to the federal party's confusion over its identity, its "conflict between dream and reality, between two incompatible positions, that of a professional opposition party and that of a party of power."[35]

Caucus looked to staff, and staff stared back. A federal election was coming, and where was the message? In 1984, Caplan and Grier had settled on "ordinary Canadians," and for months everyone had sung the same refrain. What about this time? Trade? Taxes? The "corporate agenda"?

In early June, the caucus held a final day-long retreat in the old Reading Room on Parliament Hill, where the murals on the high walls show farmers and fur traders gazing into a bright future. A dozen MPs sat at the centre of the enormous room and speculated on the coming election. Edmonston and Nystrom placed a wager on the NDP's showing. Edmonston said seven seats. Nystrom, who always hedged his bets, guessed it would be somewhere between nine and twelve. Then they said good-bye.

"Caucus was seldom used to really work out our differences, over staff or over philosphy," says Edmonston. "It boiled, and people would complain, and people would have their cathartic experiences, and then it would go down. There was no follow-through. Every caucus meeting was a psychodrama. Near the end, you were down to Svend and Fulton preaching caucus discipline. Hah! In the NDP, caucus discipline was an oxymoron."[36]

The New Democrats in Parliament worked hard and long. They agonized over their failure to win Canadians over with their message. Perhaps they were doomed to lose their seats in the 1993 election. But instead of using all available techniques to look for a solution, the caucus muddled along, mismanaged and disorganized, until the prospects for a turnaround in the party's fortunes slipped away altogether.

5

Adieu Québec

Dans la maison néo-démocrate, il n'y a pas de place pour deux nationalismes.

— Paul-André Comeau[1]

In analysing the federal NDP's election loss, the pundits and columnists look back most often to one pre-election moment: the party's decision to join the business élite on the Yes side in the 1992 constitutional referendum.

This decision — inevitably — offended some people on the other side of the referendum issue. More important, it showed the NDP riding with the élite parties rather than taking a clear position of its own on the future of Confederation. During the referendum period, the party did nothing to clarify its always confusing position on Quebec, supporting both *la société distincte* and the protection of federal government powers. It continued to baffle voters inside and outside Quebec.

Many have argued that the 1992 referendum campaign was a kind of dress-rehearsal for the federal election campaign a year later. In 1993, the parties talked about jobs, the deficit and leadership. But Canada's regions voted almost precisely according to their long-held views on central government and federalism. Francophone Quebec chose its national party. Ridings with strong federal allegiances, including Atlantic Canada, Ontario, the West Island of Montreal, and some multicultural urban ridings in the West, chose the Liberals. The Reform Party inherited most of the right-wing Tory seats in the West along with some formerly solid NDP seats, indicating a new alliance of property owners and workers opposed to bilingualism, multiculturalism and aboriginal claims. The NDP was squeezed from all sides. It did not speak for Quebec, nor could it pretend to have bridges into Quebec; it did not speak for any region, or for English Canada as a whole. Its long search for a decent compromise on Quebec-Canada relations had led nowhere.

The NDP was the first federal party to recognize Quebec as a nation, in its founding statement of 1961. It agreed to special status for Quebec starting in the late 1960s and recognized Quebec's right to independence in the early 70s. None of this cut much ice with the Quebec media, which continued to view the NDP as a centralizing party of Anglos. Their suspicion was well founded: the ideas of Frank Scott, the constitutional mentor of the CCF, continued to dominate the NDP.

Scott believed in national planning. Only a strong federal state could stand up to the major corporations; the provinces acting alone would inevitably compete for investment by driving down labour, welfare and environmental standards. Many New Democrats still have a rock-solid belief in the importance of federal standards and federal spending power — that is, the right of Ottawa to finance programs even in areas where the provinces claim jurisdiction. In the mainstream Quebec view, this centralist tendency contradicts the NDP's nominal acceptance of Quebec's special nature.

For many years, the NDP generally operated on the margins of Quebec politics. However, the work of the Parti Québécois government after 1976 showed the presence of a large social democratic electoral base in the province. The PQ introduced state auto insurance, anti-scab labour legislation and new forms of popular investment in Quebec industry.

When the PQ clamped down on government workers in the early 1980s and its separatist agenda came to an apparent dead end at the same time, a trickle of labour and social activists moved to the NDP. The long-dormant provincial NDP acquired an energetic leader, an Irish Quebecker named Jean-Paul Harney who had sat briefly as an MP for Toronto. On the federal side, leader Ed Broadbent saw a historic opportunity. One of his senior aides, George Nakitsas from Montreal, began to recruit Québécois talent. "The past was past, people were sure of themselves, and to a certain extent they wanted to play on a bigger ice rink — Canada."[2]

Outside Quebec, Broadbent engineered a fragile party-wide agreement to back the 1987 Meech Lake Accord, with its concession to Quebec's five basic demands. The NDP leader developed a warm relationship with Louis Laberge, the godfather of organized labour in Quebec, and his deputy Fernand Daoust. Nakitsas attracted star candidates — a saintly university rector in the rural north, a bank vice-president in downtown Montreal, a provincial deputy minister in Quebec City.

The 1987 federal convention in Montreal gave the NDP big-league exposure in the Quebec media, although a strike by unionized Radio-Canada technicians washed out the scheduled TV coverage. Broadbent kicked off a 90-minute debate that resulted in near-unanimous agreement on Quebec's "unique" status and the Quebec National Assembly's special responsibilities for the French language. Finally, said Montreal's Le Devoir, it seemed the NDP might be taking a "pro-Québécois direction."[3]

"There was a real opening up," says a Montreal-based activist about the visiting NDP delegates, "although nobody knew what it meant. But they said, Let's do it. We kinda like these Quebec members. They're good guys."[4] The federal NDP stood at over 30 per cent in the Quebec opinion polls, and for the first time it looked like a pan-Canadian party. The federal executive agreed to commit more than a third of the campaign advertising budget to Quebec.

In this euphoric state, the party exaggerated its short-term prospects. Three Quebec union leaders brought greetings to the convention but would not endorse the NDP. The media, the self-appointed guardians of Quebec's national spirit, remained cautious. Only 75 of the 1,300 delegates came from Quebec, and several of these spoke against the Broadbent motion because they felt it did not offer enough.

In the weeks after the visitors left Montreal, quarrels arose about who should run the show in Quebec. Harney and his provincial office, looking at the party structure in British Columbia and Saskatchewan, expected to have a free hand in planning federal activities. Another coalition stood with the federal leader's office, complaining that the provincial wing was riddled with separatists and third-raters. The pro-Ottawa camp included most of the party's anglophones, but it could not be called federalist; it included Rémi Trudel, the saintly rector, and François Beaulne, the bank vice-president, who would soon leave the New Democrats and join the PQ in the National Assembly. For now, Trudel and Broadbent formed a supreme alliance, and Trudel's organizers got licence to roam the province on the federal party's behalf. At a crucial party meeting, the pro-Ottawa side won a bitterly contested vote instructing the provincial executive to stick to provincial issues. The Quebec NDP had decapitated its own leadership.

It was a complicated time, says Nakitsas; "you couldn't tell the players without a program."[5] Michel Agnaieff, who served as the federal NDP's "associate president" for Quebec, complains that the only program was in Nakitsas' brain.

> When I reached the heights in the federal hierarchy I found myself on the committee preparing the elections. Then I found there was a steering committee. Then I found there was another committee preparing the agenda for the steering committee.
>   I reached that level, too. I was now among the very happy few. Still, the decisions were not made there. They were made around the leader's office. This is natural. What was not natural was the process of transmission of the will of the leader to the party. Those games should be played in the open ... The transmission system was very cumbersome. Things were never said clearly. I never had frank and clear discussions about what was going on in Quebec, even though I was supposed to be the number one in Quebec for a long time.[6]

The NDP continued to sign up Quebec members, and by mid-1988 claimed more than 15,000. But its electoral prospects suffered a fatal setback in autumn 1987 when the Parti Québécois announced its support for the proposed Canada-U.S. trade deal. The PQ still commanded the hearts of the labour rank and file, and its decision left pro-NDP Quebec trade unionists out on a limb. The moderate left divided; many Quebec unions, partners in a joint economic strategy with Quebec employers and government, decided to take the free-trade risk just as Swedish social democrats had in the 1950s.[7] Unions outside Quebec, fearful of being victimized by business and government, took a firmly protectionist line. In terms of their own interests, the Quebec nationalists' support for free trade was a miscalculation;[8] it also caused a bitter reaction among social democrats in English Canada, and probably ended the period of sentimental openness to Quebec in the NDP.

When the election campaign began in October 1988, the NDP in Quebec had dropped in the polls to the low 20s. Internal survey results showed the party was not seen to be "speaking for Quebec." Support slid further; Michel Agnaieff, who had split with Nakitsas, was recalled from his north Montreal campaign to help craft a nationalist appeal. On a Friday morning, seven candidates, including Harney, Agnaieff and Beaulne, announced that in supporting a "distinct society" for Quebec, the NDP recognized that Quebec's language laws took precedence over the Charter of Rights.

This was, as it turned out, the federal NDP's position. The campaign directors in Ottawa confirmed it the same day.[9] But the Montreal English media, especially *The Gazette*, reacted as if the party was "going to put everybody in concentration camps."[10] The fractured Quebec party panicked and turned on itself. A group of West Island candidates issued a counter-statement on the NDP's staunch support for English-language rights, causing a stir in the French media. In a visit to Quebec 10 days later, Ed Broadbent tried to make the issue of language rights a purely provincial matter with the memorable line, "je ne suis pas un Québécois."

Whether it was labour's support for the trade deal or its public disarray, the NDP's hopes came to naught. The party took a record 15 per cent of the Quebec vote, but it did not win seats. Disappointed candidates and their followers drifted away. The provincial wing declared independence and soon faded. Party membership in Quebec fell by half through the next year.

Quebec receded in importance within the federal party. A September 1989 meeting of the Federal Council voted to demand changes to the Meech Lake Accord. At the leadership convention a few months later in Winnipeg, just 65 delegates of a total 2,400 came from Quebec. The convention debate on Meech Lake and its "distinct society" clause resulted in what Audrey McLaughlin called "a combination of support ... and opposition."[11] Delegates voted to support Quebec's five points in the accord, but also to urge a renegotiation of the deal to provide more protection for women and aboriginal peoples. Senior CBC correspondent David Halton estimated that 75 per cent of convention delegates simply wanted to scrap Meech. By seizing the microphones and presenting a united front, federal and provincial leaders won an apparent compromise and a concession to Quebec.

Quebec was not buying. Jean-Paul Harney, now the ex-leader of the Quebec NDP, labelled the convention decision "theatre of the absurd,"[12] while *Le Devoir* concluded that the NDP had rejected the distinct society concept.[13] By summer 1990, the Quebec party's membership had fallen by half again.

Thus died the NDP's day in Quebec. Its failure undercut the NDP's hopes for taking power in Ottawa, and an anti-Quebec backlash grew up among the party rank and file. There was wide agreement that the party had squandered millions in Quebec, thanks to the 1988 campaign management team of Nakitsas, NDP federal secretary Bill Knight, and Robin Sears, the chief adviser to Ontario NDP leader Bob Rae.[14] Quebec labour had sold out Canadian workers by supporting the trade deal, probably because they wanted to break up Canada. The party's support for the Meech Lake Accord had been a mistake all along; Quebec supported Meech only as a step towards separation, part of a pattern "in which short-term manoeuvres and deliberate ambiguity veil deeper, long-term objectives."[15] The separatist agenda was destroying Canada by encouraging short-sighted premiers like Getty and Vander Zalm to claim the same new powers as Quebec.

Or perhaps, some members said, the whole separatist gambit was a hoax, a way for Quebec to extort federal loot. This view provoked at least one round of NDP questions in the Commons on special government treatment for Quebec. Quebec's largest daily pounced: the NDP had shown its true face, said the three-column headline. "En montrant son vrai visage, le NPD renonce au Québec."[16]

With Audrey McLaughlin in charge, party staff and Hill staff remained largely unilingual. When Quebec adviser Claude Rompré stormed out over Meech Lake, Audrey McLaughlin hired a replacement, but only to work in Ottawa one day a week. The new adviser, Alain Tassé, found his boss sympathetic to Quebec but reluctant to campaign openly on the party's official stand. "She was open to discussion, but it's one thing to have a philosophical discussion, and another to act."[17]

Remarkably, the NDP won a lopsided victory in the federal by-election in Chambly in January 1990. The voters told NDP canvassers, "You guys hate us, but we're voting for your candidate anyways."[18] The winner, Phil Edmonston, an American-born consumer advocate and media personality, took 68 per cent of the vote in a mostly French suburban riding southeast of Montreal. But Brian Topp, a member of the Quebec NDP's pro-Ottawa camp who came to Parliament Hill as Edmonston's assistant, says McLaughlin's unilingual staff from Manitoba declined follow up on the win.

> When Ed Broadbent left, a light went out. After we won in Chambly, Broadbent's team would have analysed the results and trained the organizers and the canvassers for the next round. Balagus and Campbell never spent two minutes on Quebec. We manoeuvred in Quebec for three years because we wanted to work with the centre [i.e., the leader's office and federal headquarters], and then the centre told us to get lost.[19]

In another federal by-election in mid-1990 in Montreal, the NDP got less than a third of its 1988 vote share. By 1993, the party was scrambling to find enough undergraduates to fill its Quebec slate, and it earned less than 2 per cent of the vote. The NDP's combination of centralist dogmatism and Western bias, says Brian Topp, had overruled its political interests. Like much of Canada outside Quebec, the NDP accepted the words *distinct society*, but rejected the reality. "We demanded a centralized state and rejected federalism. This was a test of maturity for the Canadian left, and it failed. The available common ground was a federal state, and not a unitary state based in Ottawa."[20]

John Richards, the B.C.-based economist, agrees.

The Tories could do it. The Chamber of Commerce guy in Red Deer who voted Tory had no more love for the "frogs" in Quebec than the IWA guy in Nanaimo. But the Tories understood that they couldn't remain a Western-based Anglo party, which they had become under Diefenbaker. They had the discipline to say to the Red Deer candidate and the Chicoutimi candidate, you've got to work out something if we're going to be a governing party. You can't go on ignoring each other.[21]

Michel Agnaieff adds: "For a party that has a reputation as a tenacious party, defending its principles, when you look inside the NDP the word that describes it best is impatience. If you invest in Quebec, they thought, you have to get quick returns."[22]

McLaughlin's party, for obvious reasons, came to view the Canada-Quebec issue as a nuisance. And when the Mulroney government announced yet another constitutional round, the NDP in Ottawa reacted with something like despair. More constitutional talks would divert attention from the issues the NDP favoured and deliver nothing in return. Council of Canadians chair Maude Barlow predicted that because the NDP was "afraid to talk about Quebec," it would remain "a minor player in the upcoming negotiations."[23] The party's standing in the polls was sure to drop significantly.

Mulroney had promised that the "Canada round" would contain something for everyone — Quebec, the West, big business, the provinces, women and aboriginal peoples. McLaughlin, Les Campbell and senior MPs considered boycotting the process, but decided the NDP could not sit on the sidelines for 18 months. The leader elected to build the NDP position on non-Quebec issues, and she unveiled its basic design in February 1991 in a luncheon speech at the Château Laurier. McLaughlin drew repeated and prolonged applause from her audience, made up of MPs and Parliament Hill staff who had been called out for a free meal in front of the cameras.

She raised three issues. First, since Canadians had disliked Meech Lake's back-room origins, she revived an idea that had floated around the NDP for some years — that the Constitution should be referred to a special citizens' parliament, or constituent assembly. (McLaughlin did not provide details, then or later, of the assembly's make-up or powers.) Second, the NDP would promote the inherent right of aboriginal peoples to self-government. Third, the NDP would demand the inclusion of a social charter in the Constitution.

The NDP also wanted a new understanding with Quebec. But if the Conservative and Liberal positions were self-contradictory, the New Democrat position was more so: distinct status for Quebec, and yet an unyielding defence of national standards and the federal spending power. John Richards, in a harsh written commentary, says the NDP's stand on Quebec-Canada relations rested on a passive hope for compromise and no hard detail, "a naïve faith in the goodness of men — and of women ... Such faith induces political leaders to avoid the painful exercise of constraining and reconciling conflicting interests, and without the careful balancing of political interests the result is anarchic chaos."[24]

Twice in the 1980s Ed Broadbent had agreed to federal constitutional projects without consulting the party. McLaughlin resolved to act differently. She would strike a large, active party committee representing all regions and interests. This body would advise her and the MPs on how to proceed in Parliament, and help explain caucus decisions to the membership. McLaughlin also proposed a special party convention on the Constitution, but was persuaded that it would get lost in a traffic jam of federal, provincial, aboriginal and private-sector meetings and hearings. The party committee met for the first time in Montreal, to show the NDP's continued interest in Quebec; it elected co-chairs, and reporters quizzed McLaughlin on remarks that Phil Edmonston had let slip the day before. All subsequent meetings were held in Ottawa.

After its early reluctance, the NDP now put increasing energy into the constitutional exercise. The caucus was entitled to three members on the new Parliamentary Committee on the Constitution; McLaughlin named five. Lorne Nystrom, the caucus constitution critic, persuaded the other parties to let all five attend meetings and question witnesses, although only three NDP MPs would sign the final report. Nystrom hired two legislative experts and got the full-time use of a caucus researcher, while Campbell brought me over from the office of Joy Langan, MP, to monitor events and prepare reports for party members and labour.

Campbell felt the NDP should set an independent course and avoid a final accord with the Liberals and Conservatives. The problem with this, of course, was the NDP's lack of a distinctive position on Quebec- Canada relations; it was accustomed to following the others, and "hoping for the best."[25] Campbell's idea was doomed; Lorne Nystrom had little regard for Campbell or his strategy, and he had far more influence with caucus than the leader's assistant. He was confident that he had the skill and the stature to win concessions from the government in the back rooms and put the NDP's stamp on the final constitutional package. Barricaded in his office just upstairs from McLaughlin's, Nystrom ran his own constitutional headquarters, a clubhouse that welcomed MPs, federal officials and the occasional courier from the leader's office.

Elected in 1968 from Saskatchewan, Lorne Nystrom lived with his wife and children in Aylmer, Quebec, and shared many of the concerns of the liberal, bilingual Anglo-Quebecker. He placed a high priority on settling with Quebec, and appeared bound from the first to sign an all-party final report. He got strong support from several Ontario MPs who said voters would punish the NDP for playing partisan politics with this issue. As an appointed trouble-spotter, I advised the leader that the party was being dragged into a Tory melodrama, but I saw no alternative.

> The caucus has the option of signing on with a discredited majority, or risking public exposure on a number of controversial and divisive issues. It is my sense that the majority in our group will lean towards an accommodation with an all-party position, not least because of the lack of clarity within the party on both Quebec and Senate reform.[26]

Armed with the proxy votes of three NDP provincial premiers, Nystrom beat the government back on the pro-business agenda put forward by Constitutional Affairs Minister Joe Clark. The Conservatives withdrew their property rights proposal, eliminated a reactionary definition of the Bank of Canada, killed the mysterious

Council of the Federation, and gutted some potentially anti–public ownership language on interprovincial trade.

Nystrom did not, however, try to block the proposal to create an elected Senate despite the NDP's long-held position that the Senate should be abolished. Premiers Harcourt and Romanow had yielded to Western public opinion on this question, even if it provoked discontent among New Democrats. When McLaughlin's party advisory committee met for the second time, Gerald Caplan of Ontario complained that the new Senate would be expensive and partisan, and would "paralyse the whole goddamn system ... we've been hijacked with an idea that simply doesn't make sense." If ever there was crass vote-buying, said Caplan, this was it. What was the value of having a party committee if the whole exercise was driven by realpolitik? [27]

Caplan raised an important question. For the most part, the NDP premiers ignored McLaughlin's federal party committee. In seven or eight meetings, nobody ever attended from British Columbia. Saskatchewan delegate Sandra Mitchell appeared once or twice, but Premier Romanow made it clear he thought constitutional reform was an issue for the premiers and the prime minister to sort out. Caplan attended for Ontario, but more as an eminent social democrat than as an envoy of Bob Rae. McLaughlin's committee, then, was a flawed early warning system for a federal leader operating at the edge the Constitutional storm system, faithfully supported by the weak client parties of Atlantic Canada. It offered a place to the labour rep, the women's rep, the youth rep, the aboriginal rep and (until he stormed out in a scrap over the Charter of Rights) the visible minorities rep. Convening each month in a different hotel room, the committee waded diligently through the issues, usually concluding without enthusiasm that Nystrom's all-party compromises in Parliament offered the best available course. The group took the initiative on just one issue: the definition of a constitutional social charter.

McLaughlin's agenda was holding up fairly well. The constituent assembly idea had died, but Nystrom and McLaughlin had persuaded Joe Clark to fund a series of five independently run constitutional conferences. The inherent right to aboriginal self-government was on track, with Clark's support. The social charter concept had attracted favourable comment from party members, social activists and the media. It was popular enough, in fact, that McLaughlin and Bob Rae were jostling to take credit.

As Maude Barlow put it, the inspiration for a social charter had come from the Europeans, who recognized the need for common ground rules on social services. "The Europeans recognize ... that unless there is specific government action to prevent it, corporations will use their new-found mobility to force a competitive reduction of living standards among competing nations. The Europeans have, with the social charter, declared such competition 'illegal.' "[28]

Midway through January 1992, I went to Les Campbell to suggest that it was time to give some shape to the hazy social charter proposal. Campbell had the same idea. Two weeks later, the party committee agreed that the Constitution should oblige federal and provincial governments to work for the following: full employment and fair working conditions, income security, socialized health care, the provision of food and shelter, quality education and a clean environment. Progress would be monitored either by a panel of elected senators or by a commission of experts. The committee advised McLaughlin to make the proposal public.

The leader then consulted NDP human rights critic Howard McCurdy. After his predictable explosion of fury at not having been consulted he insisted on an important caveat: there would be no suggestion that the courts might enforce the social charter, now or ever. He did not want to see judges designing government programs from the bench.

On February 6, McLaughlin sat down at the National Press Theatre to release her social charter proposal, her first formal statement on the Constitution in several months. Premier Rae, nudged out of a long silence by McLaughlin's statement, came forward with a similar list 10 days later. To the surprise of many New Democrats, the Mulroney government offered a package almost immediately. The Constitution would list government "commitments" to health, education, social services, the environment and — a late entry from NDP President Nancy Riche — the right of workers or organize and bargain collectively. For the first time, it appeared, the Constitution would provide at least rhetorical support for the welfare state.

Nothing was certain, however, in this obstinately long Constitutional round. Through the summer doldrums of 1991, the media had mused on the shape of upcoming events. Then we had the parliamentary phase, six months of negotiation and pseudo-crisis that produced an all-party report one hour after the midnight deadline on February 26, 1992. Then nine provincial governments took charge; their officials spent six months crossing Canada with aboriginal leaders, shuffling constitutional furniture. Premier Bourassa and his government jumped in at the last minute with their list of demands; in the view of B.C. minister Moe Sihota, trumpeted during the referendum, Quebec played its cards badly, and lost, and then everyone signed an accord at Charlottetown on August 28.

For the federal NDP, the process represented a virtual media blackout and a political dead end, and the worst was yet to come. The morning after Charlottetown, 100 members of the Federal Council met in a large, low-ceilinged room in the basement of the Château Laurier. McLaughlin and Premier Rae made stirring speeches, telling delegates that the accord represented a great victory for aboriginal peoples and perhaps the last chance at an agreement among Canada's regions. In discussion, one or two speakers expressed qualms; but excited by the NDP gains and loyal to their leaders, the delegates voted without dissent in support of the accord.

A week later, the NDP caucus went a step further. In a retreat at the elegant Gray Rocks resort in the Laurentians, the MPs decided to join the Liberals and Conservatives in the national campaign to sell the Charlottetown Accord. The polls showed 67 per cent public support for the deal, 20 against.[29] McLaughlin had been assured that the Yes committee would include the provincial governments, the territories and the aboriginal groups.

The key discussion came at a Saturday lunch of the caucus executive and senior party officials. Michael Balagus, McLaughlin's communications director, told the group it would be crazy to campaign alongside the big parties. He was so loud and so dogged that McLaughlin scolded him in front of the others. Les Campbell says when the vote came, "Michael was the only one who voted against. That put a lot of backs up — him presuming to vote. There was more agreement and less controversy at that meeting than most of the others I attended."[30]

The "Canada round" negotiations and the Charlottetown Accord offered something for every Canadian — something to oppose, that is. Even so, the margin of loss in the referendum was fairly narrow: 54.4 per cent to 45.6 per cent. Without Brian Mulroney and his promise to crush "the enemies of Canada," and without the Yes committee's TV ads, the accord might have carried Canada outside Quebec. But the Yes camp's sensational $6.2 million campaign backfired, with its insistence that voters must save the country from a crisis created by politicians. Many people were pleased to let the politicians dig their own graves.

The NDP had no control over Mulroney, but it played an eager and active part in the Yes campaign, because, for a period of six weeks, it was the only political game in town. Les Campbell, once the harshest critic of working with the bigger parties, went to work on the phones at the Yes shop, along with a clutch of party and parliamentary staff.

McLaughlin phoned Gerald Caplan and asked him to act as the federal party's senior delegate to the Yes committee. Caplan says he tried to shy away. "I was ambivalent, and not sure I knew what the federal party's position was. I suggested she should appoint a woman." However, Caplan says McLaughlin insisted that he act as her "direct representative."

Each morning Caplan and former federal secretary Bill Knight joined Campbell at the Yes campaign meetings and wrestled with the likes of Conservative Hugh Segal and Liberal Senator Michael Kirby. However, Campbell and Balagus organized McLaughlin's work for the Yes side without consulting Caplan or Knight. Caplan found out about McLaughlin's television debate with Preston Manning after it had been scheduled; his screaming match with Balagus ended their relationship.[31]

As it turned out, McLaughlin's debate with Manning was a rare bright moment for the NDP. Manning had never faced any opposition as Reform leader, and she reduced him to human scale. However, there were no further debates between the two, perhaps because some in the party felt it would give Manning too much credibility as a force on the national scene.

McLaughlin toured Canada for the Yes side. "She went on every radio talk show in Western Canada," says one assistant, "and everywhere she went, she got crucified. People would phone and say, 'I've always supported your party, but you and Mulroney are giving the country away to Quebec.' They'd come up to her on the street and say, 'We've given them too much already. Let them go.' Of course Audrey took this personally, and that just made it all worse." Even the crowd at the Winnipeg Union Centre turned hostile, and local MP Bill Blaikie shook with emotion as he tried to explain the compromise.

"They were selling Mulroney's agenda, and it was a bad agenda," says political scientist Daniel Drache. "And they were getting very little in return. The price for Charlottetown should have been no to free trade ... There was a kind of absence of a bottom line for the NDP. They never seem to come to these issues with policies that let them say, We get this or we're out."[32]

"The Liberals took a low profile," says Michael Balagus. "More importantly, they were expected to be on the Yes side. They didn't disappoint anybody. In politics, if you do what people expect you to do, you stay out of trouble."[33] People did not expect the NDP to get into bed with Mulroney, and MPs who conducted local pro-Yes campaigns to prepare their local machines for the coming election soon found themselves fighting with party members. They also found, in the words of an NDP activist who is also a constitutional scholar, that many long-time New Democrats "hate Quebec and they hate Indians."[34]

"We didn't have any choice but to support the Charlottetown Accord," says Saskatoon MP Chris Axworthy. "We were more tolerant than the average Canadian, and tolerance is what is going to hold this country together. Most people didn't care, or they were perplexed enough that they couldn't see holding the country together as being worth all the compromises they were asked to make."[35]

The referendum came, and voters rejected the Charlottetown Accord and the work that went into it. What does that say about the NDP's contribution?

The televised consitutional conferences, a concession to McLaughlin's concerns about process, did not influence the politicians' document. The conferences probably served to raise cynicism rather than dampen it.

The aboriginals' inherent right of self-government became a mainstream concept, but the Liberal Party picked up most of the credit. While Liberal critic Ethel Blondin-Andrew toured aboriginal communities before the referendum, NDP critic Bob Skelly stuck to his riding. When Grand Chief Ovide Mercredi met with the NDP caucus, he scolded the MPs for their low profile on the issue, and held up Blondin-Andrew as a shining example. In March 1994, the Liberal government announced it would dismantle the Department of Indian Affairs and work for aboriginal self-government.

The social charter is gone. It may be resurrected in a future constitutional round. But as a staff propagandist for the idea, I would caution against making it a make-or-break priority.

The charter promised to build a welfare state vision into one corner of the Constitution. New Democrats were thrilled when the

Conservatives conceded its validity. Doubts remain, however, about whether it would have had any real effect. The European charter has no force in law; it does not make anything "illegal," as Barlow argued, or "guarantee" anything, as Audrey McLaughlin claimed in her book.[36] Putting it in the worst light, legal scholar Michael Mandel suggests that the social charter proposal is a smokescreen that allows social democrats to substitute rhetoric for action.

> As the Ontario social charter document admits: "Jurisdiction over most of Canada's social policy domains is in provincial hands." What does this mean? It means that everything the Rae government calls for in the social charter is something that it has the full right not only to "guarantee" but to actually *deliver* to the people of Ontario *right now*. Name the goal, and, as far as the constitution is concerned, Bob Rae's government has the right to achieve it. Ontario can raise the minimum wage, open closing plants, restore jobs and provide a decent standard of living to the record numbers on Ontario's welfare rolls. Of course, the government would have to get very tough with big business to make it all possible ...[37]

After an enormous (and somewhat dishonest) detour around the Quebec question during the "Canada round," the challenge of redefining Canada-Quebec relations still sits squarely in front of us — the challenge that drove the constitutional agenda through the 1960s, 70s and 80s.

Recent opinion polls show that Quebec francophones favour sovereignty, although the meaning of this term is unclear. A majority of Québécois voted for sovereigntist candidates in the 1993 federal election. Many institutions of the Québécois left, drawing together trade unionists, social action groups, artists and thinkers, are active in the pro-sovereignty movement.

One aspect of the NDP's divided psyche wants to respect Quebec's hopes. Another feels Quebec's unending demands have distracted and divided Canada. In the past, the NDP has bridged this tension by keeping Quebec's cultural and economic demands in separate rhetorical compartments. Yes, the NDP supports protection for the French language; but what Quebec really needs, said Tommy Douglas, is the reassurance provided by jobs and prosperity. Audrey McLaughlin wants to find "the building blocks for a country we're sure Quebec will want to remain part of, the country we all want to be part of."[38]

The sovereigntists certainly want jobs for Quebec. But more than that, they want control — partly to fulfil a nationalist dream, and partly because they see Canada drifting towards disintegration.

The NDP agreed long ago that Quebec has the right to control its future. It is now time for social democrats outside Quebec to think this through, especially given that their leftist counterparts in Quebec support sovereignty. The status quo, which consists of endless bickering over the joint Constitution, is no longer an option. Canadians outside Quebec must agree either to a meaningful form of special status for Quebec or to separation.

The special status option might take many forms. Lorne Nystrom supports administrative agreements: maintain the symbolic unity of Canada while Quebec runs social and economic programs. Aboveground, governments could work towards constitutional amendments one at a time, as they do in the United States. Below ground, Ottawa could sign away control over programs to Quebec or any other province without surrendering formal jurisdiction.[39] This plan assumes that Quebec nationalism is a façade for bureaucratic ambition in Quebec City, an assumption that may not stand up.

Action Canada, the Ottawa-based coalition of social action groups and organized labour, has called for an openly "asymmetrical federalism," as have some New Democrat fragments. Quebec would gain jurisdiction in some areas now controlled by Ottawa, and in return would surrender influence in Parliament and the federal government. This idea would be fully as complex in its application as outright separation, but it would keep Quebec under the Canadian flag. "Asymmetrical federalism" won some converts in the televised public conferences, but the politicians never took it seriously.

The chances that Quebec will win special status within Canada appear remote at this time. Several premiers insisted before the referendum that there could be "no special deals for Quebec," and sold many voters on the reality of "equality of the provinces." Even a minor concession promising Quebec 25 per cent of the seats in the Commons is credited with driving many Westerners to the No side. Positions on both sides of the Canada-Quebec divide are growing increasingly hardline.

I will propose here that the federal NDP, as a Canadian party, should work to define Canadian priorities. Where these differ from Quebec's priorities, the NDP should not try to hide the differences.

The NDP does not have the enthusiasm among its members, the resources at its Ottawa head office, or, I would argue, the historical mandate, to rebuild a social democratic party in Quebec. Most of its one-time target group in Quebec now views the NDP as a colonizing force.

The two nations are on divergent paths. In the labour movement, the credit union movement, the farmer's movement and much of the women's movement, Quebec and Canadian components already operate at arm's length. They share many objectives, but the Quebec organizations run their own programs and fashion their own political links within the province and with Ottawa. If, for electoral purposes, Quebec social democrats choose to ride with their conservative nationalist pals as they have in the past, so be it. If they choose to form their own party, the NDP should be prepared to consider an alliance.

Paradoxically, the NDP's attempts to balance between Canadian federalism and Quebec nationalism have done nothing for national unity. While the party chases a nationalist Quebec base, it limits its freedom to expose the dishonesty of many sovereigntist promises. Former B.C. party secretary Gerry Scott says the NDP must speak for its members and its constituency in frank discussions with the left in Quebec.

We should get the hell out of Quebec. We shouldn't run candidates there. We should go there frequently as the English-Canadian left, saying, Here's the way we see federalism. Here's our approach to what you want, which you call sovereignty. That doesn't include Mr. Parizeau's idea of having two passports. We have to be very firm about that. In order that we can be good neighbours and live in understanding, they have to be aware — in fairness — that we're not interested in their having two passports. [40]

In a 1994 interview, Audrey McLaughlin rejected this line of thinking. She said the Canada-Quebec issue would continue to be a "horror show" for the NDP. However, she says the party should maintain its presence in Quebec.

Once again, the NDP will probably be drawn into something over which we have absolutely no control, and have to take some position. It is the worst of all worlds. It's one thing to take a position and have some influence; it's another to take a position and have no influence.

I know that there is, in some quarters, a feeling that the party should just forget about Quebec. Maybe it's part of questioning the need for a federal party. At the moment, I am not in any way prepared to say that Quebec is a lost cause ... I don't think you put a lot of resources into it, because it's not our time. And as you say, most of the left and labour are into the sovereigntist movement. But you don't know what's going to happen. Every person I talk to, unless they're Bloc Québécois MPs, says the referendum may not pass ... [41]

If the sovereignty referendum fails, optimists in the Quebec NDP believe Quebec social democrats could come rushing back to the NDP as they did in the mid-1980s.

On the other hand, there may be a Yes vote for sovereignty, now or in the future. This is not a development Canadians will welcome. "One should not overestimate the power of emotion in national breakups of the type we are contemplating: the desire to do injury or exact revenge may well outweigh any cost-benefit analysis."[42] So what is the best response to this possibility — to dismiss it as unthinkable, or to draw up a plan?

Daniel Drache, editor of the 1992 book *Negotiating with a Sovereign Quebec*, argues that the NDP and other Canadian institutions have a responsibility to prepare for negotiations. The list of items to be negotiated is long. Beyond sawing the debt in two, Quebec and Canada would have to agree on military, banking and environmental arrangements, and on self-government for aboriginal peoples in Quebec. Drache says the alternative to preparedness is panic — or, at the very best, a Canadian agenda prepared by the Business Council on National Issues. McLaughlin, on the other hand, says the federal NDP will not influence the outcome of any negotiations with Quebec.

We are not going to be on a committee. We do not have clout in Quebec. We do not have the members of Parliament ... The provinces are a different matter. If we are still in government, that becomes pertinent.

If they decide to leave, well, we'll deal with that. But what do you mean by a contingency plan? A plan on trading arrangements, or on currency? There isn't a government in Canada that

would say, Oh, that's okay, it'll be all right. I know that's what
the Bloc wants to tell people, but the anger in the rest of Canada
would be huge.[43]

If there is anger in Canada, or a desire for a reasonable settlement
with Quebec, how will it be expressed? Through what agency? The
federal government, as McLaughlin suggests? Speaking on behalf of
whom? The provincial governments? Speaking for whose vision of
Canada?

The NDP can choose among many options on the Quebec question, none of them comfortable. It can hope for the problem to go
away, stay on the sidelines, or echo what the Liberals say, the familiar courses that helped bring on the electoral disaster of 1993. If the
party wants to regain support among Quebec social democrats, it
must offer Quebec a form of autonomy within Confederation. This
is my own off-beat preference, but I fear it would have limited appeal
in Ontario, and less in the West. If the NDP wishes to speak for its
membership and its long-time constituency, I believe it must develop
a distinctive, pro-Canadian position that includes an honest bargaining position on Quebec sovereignty.

Perhaps the imminent prospect of Quebec separation will persuade
Canadians to accept Quebec autonomy or asymmetry. Or perhaps
Canadians will decide that their chances for survival and prosperity
would actually improve with Quebec's departure, and that Canada
would then have the freedom to focus on its own future — and, of
course, the future of the many aboriginal nations, dozens (or hundreds?) of them, whose constitutional status also remains unresolved.

6

Dreams and Economics

The party is loved for its heart, but not its brain.
— Gerald Caplan[1]

I like the warm feeling you get in a church like the NDP, but I don't like the intellectually numbing consequences. It's very hard when people think they know the truth and the truth is unchanging ... The NDP has been pretty weak at understanding profound changes in society that have to be responded to.
— James Laxer[2]

The NDP's first television advertisements in the 1993 campaign followed the party tradition of dividing society into "Us" and "Them." The ads showed knots of enraged citizens shouting at each other or the camera about the evils of an economic system run by "Them," also known in NDP polling language as "powerful corporations and the wealthy." The ads fit with Audrey McLaughlin's speeches, which mentioned corporations only in the context of tax evasion and political corruption. They recalled Us-and-Them slogans from previous campaigns — "standing with ordinary Canadians," "we're on your side," "people like us."

The party also had a Jobs Plan document, released in February 1993, which proposed in part that government should work with "Them" to promote training, research and job creation. With this plan, the NDP had attempted for the first time in many years to increase its credibility on economic issues. However, the document had too little impact, even among Canadians on the left, to matter in the election.

In a campaign where concerns about jobs and the deficit determined many votes, the NDP staggered under its reputation for economic illiteracy. The party's response, as in the 1988 election, was to flee the major issue of the day and focus on saving medicare, taxing the rich, and exposing the Liberals' corporate links. An Insight

Canada post-election poll asked 1,083 people which party was closest to them on "the economy generally"; 51 per cent chose the Liberals, 14 per cent Reform, 10 per cent the Bloc, 6 per cent the Conservatives, and 1 per cent the NDP. On jobs and unemployment, rated by half those polled as the leading issue, economic or non-economic, 61 per cent chose the Liberals, 4 per cent the NDP.[3]

The federal NDP had failed over time to establish an identity as a social democratic party. It had fudged the nuts-and-bolts issues of economic management. In its campaigns, the NDP offered a mishmash of populism and naïve socialism: "The owners and managers of capital and their political flunkies are bad; average Canadians [without quibbling about whom that includes] are good. We're good, too. Vote NDP." In this persona, the NDP regards the productive engine of the economy as self-powered and self-reproducing; the economic role of government is to protect workers and the environment from the engine's handlers, and to punish the handlers with high taxes. It is a world-view that leaves most voters cold; it fosters an unexamined Marxism among those who remain, and makes it far more likely the party's militants will oppose the actions of NDP governments.

The 1993 Jobs Plan brought the party's other side, its social democratic side, to the surface. Some of its contents had appeared in previous party documents; but taken together, it represented a shift for the federal NDP. The Plan asked, How can we generate jobs and pay for social programs? The answer came back: not primarily by raising taxes, not by running the federal deficit higher, but through public and private investment aimed at making Canada smarter and more productive. Canadians can only maintain decent incomes by producing goods and services the world wants to buy; that will come only through a broadly based process of ongoing innovation. A progressive social democratic government would challenge the culture of Canadian business; it would also help to form new partnerships among government, business, labour and the community.

Will this social democratic voice prevail in the party after the disaster of 1993? Or will strategists continue to look for populist updrafts at election time?

The Us-and-Them approach has a tenacious hold on the federal party, and understandably so. First, its rhetoric has emotional appeal, unlike charts and graphs on industrial policy. Second, it links the party to the CCF and a historic mission, even if the CCF's early ideas no longer apply. "There is a tendency in this country for some people who have little sympathy with socialism, and should be termed 'social democrats,' to take on the label 'socialist' as a badge of honour or out of respect for tradition."[4]

Third, if the NDP replaces "we're on your side" with a detailed agenda for government, it will mean giving some interests priority over others. This will threaten solidarity among regions, public- and private-sector workers, First Nations and environmental groups. It is less troublesome for various movements and causes to let right-wing business run the country and then react with collective outrage. When critics grumble that the NDP is an interest-group network rather than a social democratic party, it is precisely this politically driven paralysis they have in mind. "Coalition politics is built around opposition to the corporate agenda. It is not built around support for social democracy or a strengthened labour movement. It is, after all, easier to unite around a platform of opposition than one of specific change."[5]

A fourth reason for the dominance of Us and Them is that the NDP's social democratic alternatives are poorly understood in the party, as well as incomplete. There are few points of contact between the NDP's strategic hub, which concentrates on coining slogans and buying ads, and the thinkers inside and outside the party. "It's hard to see where the NDP has invested in any economic problem," says political scientist Daniel Drache. "Have they ever decided to spend $200,000 or $300,000 to commission people to do a series of studies? No. You have to put in money if you believe in it. And that's something the Liberals do."[6]

Doug Coupar, of the Canadian Labour Congress's political action committee, says the NDP has waited for labour to do the work of developing an economic program, and labour has waited for the NDP. "There is a serious and deep void in the labour movement in the area of economic policy, and I'm talking about fundamental understanding of how economies work and what we want our economy to do ... We're talking about a crisis of intellectual poverty that is just beginning to be understood by labour leaders and by people in the tattered remains of the NDP."[7]

Social democrats have long accepted the reality of a mixed economy, where state, private and co-operative players each provide benefits in their own way. The NDP's economic positions are somewhat better developed than Drache and Coupar suggest; the party has experience in government in four provinces and the Yukon, and the outlines of a partial federal strategy in the Jobs Plan. But the federal

NDP has yet to bridge the contradictions between its policy documents and its 20-second campaign clips.

At the provincial level, NDP governments have set a moderate social democratic course. Their records illustrate the strengths and weaknesses of the social democratic option for Canada. The Saskatchewan NDP, for example, governing from 1971 to 1982 under Allan Blakeney, often angered socialists and environmentalists, but it delivered quality social programs and jobs to people in the mainstream.

Like the earlier CCF administration in Saskatchewan, the NDP did not run deficits. The federal party lost sight of this fact for many years, during a period when public-sector unionists in particular viewed any discussion of the public debt as reactionary. Blakeney believed deficits to be anti-progressive, "a huge annual transfer of income from wage and salary earners, from whom most taxes are collected, to the owners of government securities."[8] In a 1994 speech, Blakeney again called deficits "a steady transfer of wealth from the earners to the owners," and said that conservative administrations in Saskatchewan, Alberta and Ottawa had run up large debts "so that future governments could be crippled."[9]

The Saskatchewan government paid for better health care and education from increased revenues, partly by attracting private investment, for example in oil production, and partly through profitable state investment in oil and potash. Blakeney later wrote that NDP governments should do more to build productive economies through active industrial programs. "In the last fifty years we have concentrated primarily on distributive justice … When we look at the actual policies of NDP governments, the emphasis has consistently been on how wealth and power are distributed rather than how they are produced."[10]

Roy Romanow returned the Saskatchewan NDP to power in 1991 with a promise to generate jobs — partly by making the private sector more profitable. Audrey McLaughlin made the following rare observation during her 1993 Jobs Plan tour: "We're not out to destroy business, we're out to make it better for small businesses and larger corporations."[11] In 1994, the Harcourt government in British Columbia engineered a social democratic plan to keep the forest industry profitable and create jobs in the process. The agreement, worked out with companies, labour, environmental groups and aboriginal groups, will channel $2 billion in forest industry revenues into conservation and renewal. It will also increase the influence of local communities and non-corporate interests over the operation of British Columbia's biggest resource industry.

Some academic and trade union critics reject Canadian social democracy in practice, calling it a timid or lazy or corrupt surrender to the capitalist order. This criticism, viewed in a positive light, helps to remind social democrats of the monstrous tendencies in capitalism. Where the market system has been tamed, it has generated the highest standard of living in history, measured by such basics as health, housing and life expectancy, although huge inequalities remain. Where it slips its leash, capitalism has a habit of devouring its environment, it workers and its customers. In a 1985 interview, the 80-year-old Tommy Douglas expressed his fear that the predatory qualities of capitalism would win a final victory.

It's not impossible to imagine a fascist world ... We may wake up some day to realize that it's not impossible on this North American continent particularly, where financial power is so highly concentrated in so few hands, with all the media for propaganda in the same hands, and with the forces of democracy divided and scattered and diffused ... We are just deceiving ourselves if we think that automatically the new world of social democracy will just evolve. It won't just evolve. It's going to be a struggle.[12]

Social democracy accepts that for the foreseeable future there will be a struggle or tension between the public interest and private or corporate centres of capital. This is different from orthodox socialism, which proposes to end the tension by smashing private control of capital in the public interest. Socialism, according to two prominent Canadian theorists, is about "taking capital away from the capitalists, and democratizing control over the instruments and process of production, distribution, and communications ..." So how do we democratize industry? For many years, socialists favoured state takeover, but this solution has lost its glamour even among Marxists. Instead, write Professors Panitch and Swartz, we should prepare to replace capitalism with *institutions that do not yet exist*. Anything else is the "politics of compromise."[13]

Canadian socialists perform a service in keeping alive the ideal of a society free from competition and greed. This ideal has great sentimental power, especially among students and among social activists in non-profit groups. It is more uplifting than the grubby reality of social democracy at work. On the other hand, it ignores some basic data from the real world, such as the desire of consumers to have choices. In an economy where the consumer is allowed a choice, even the most socialist of community enterprises and worker co-ops will be forced to compete with each other, partly by keeping wages in check and by imposing performance standards on workers. When hard-line socialists turn from denouncing capitalism to drawing up near-term blueprints for Canada, they run up against the need to build centres of profit into their plans. Sam Gindin, the Canadian Auto Workers research director, begins his economic testament with a promise to "confront capital in a radical way," and is soon building networks of private firms.[14]

The European social democratic parties have worked to develop a politics of compromise since the 1950s. Their governments have introduced steps to enhance both industrial production and social programs. In general, their economic agenda has not found much favour on the Canadian left, even though Ed Broadbent, the federal NDP's long-time leader, was a friend of many of the leading innovators in Europe.

As the Marxists point out, the Europeans have not created a worker's paradise; nevertheless, they have generated rising wages and kept unemployment low, at some cost to the individual's chances for sudden riches. Organized labour in Sweden and Germany worked out a social contract with government and business that was designed to protect wages and pension levels for as many citizens as possible, control inflation and maintain labour peace. The Swedes traded off job security for retraining and relocation programs, realizing they needed a flexible economy in order to meet each new wave of technological change. Workers in many countries have adapted to the open trading environment of the emerging European Union. They have made less progress in expanding worker and community influence in the firm and at the stock exchange.

Canada's NDP has frowned on talk of social contracts, labour mobility strategies, open trade or labour-management partnerships. From the 1960s until the 1990s, the party focused its economic attention on the actions of the Department of Finance. If Ottawa spent money at the right time and kept interest rates low, government and business could both create jobs, which would generate taxes, which would pay for social programs. Canadian industry's advantages came naturally, because of resources or location, but if a company lacked those advantages or squandered them, and made skunky wine or leaky boots, government could always offer industrial grants or block imports, and save the workers' jobs. Labour's task was to win benefits for its members; it had no responsibility for efficiency or quality. The NDP argued earnestly for Canadian ownership of private industry, but it had little to say about how to put Canadian firms or sectors on the leading edge in a changing world economy.

As long ago as 1983, NDP research director James Laxer warned that the weak Canadian manufacturing sector was breaking down despite the government protection. He urged the party to "rethink the economy" in light of experience in Europe. "NDP spokesmen have often appeared to be the last defenders of an economic system that is in decline — demanding that it live up to its former greatness. The touchstone of NDP economic thought has been the encouragement of consumption rather than production. In an era in which the nation's productive system is rapidly disintegrating, this message is very dated."[15]

Instead of rethinking the economy, the party concentrated on building a populist image. The "standing up for ordinary Canadians" appeal renewed the party's emotional link with a large group of voters and is given credit for saving some seats. However, it only delayed the day of reckoning on the economic front. The NDP continued its lopsided defence of the traditions of the welfare state, and became increasingly a party from a past era.

The 1988 free trade debate, as leftists and liberals recognized at the time, was a watershed for Canada. The Mulroney-Reagan deal restricted the power of Canadian governments to act in the public interest. It would bar Ottawa or any province from screening takeovers by U.S.-based companies or demanding job guarantees. It guaranteed "national treatment" for all companies doing business in Canada, erasing any distinction between American and Canadian firms for tax or public investment purposes.

The deal's six-month escape clause offered slight consolation. As Laxer puts it, "If you try to abrogate a deal with a superpower, you're far worse off than you were before the deal was made. There's no doubt that the top levels of American and Canadian capital would go completely crazy."[16]

The major CLC unions spent large amounts of money to alert the public to the dangers of the trade deal; Robert White's Auto Workers organized seminars for members, mailed out flyers, and ran two-page ads in 42 dailies raising concern about "social programs, environment, regional assistance, energy, privatization, deregulation, etc., in other words, not a narrow self-interest approach."[17] In a January 1988 letter to Broadbent, an economist from the labour-nationalist coalition against the deal urged the NDP to join the movement. Duncan Cameron proposed study sessions for party activists in every region and forums for the public with party leaders.[18] Even if the NDP could not win the election, it could raise the level of debate and educate party supporters on a fundamental economic issue.

Cameron's plan was never put into effect. When the election came, most New Democrat candidates were not ready to address this complex issue in plain English. Critics complained that the NDP was falling back on mindless protectionism, the defence of jobs and obsolete industries. "It was not a reasoned response that provided credible alternatives."[19] New Democrats had not studied industrial strategy and were speechless in the face of a deal that threatened to tie the hands of future social democratic governments.

By the late 1980s, NDP economics as outlined in the Commons and party pamphlets still relied on the Keynesian chain: government spending and cheap credit would create jobs, and the newly employed would boost government revenues and support social programs. Asked about the rising federal deficit, the NDP responded: Stimulate the economy, increase government revenues. The NDP also proposed tax reform, with higher tax rates for high-income earners and fewer tax deductions for business. "They were just interested in using limited Keynesian taxation measures to redistribute wealth. They thought if you had social programs, that was enough. They were wrong."[20]

When three provinces elected NDP provincial governments in the early 1990s, many Canadians expected them to govern according to the formulas the federal party had used in opposition. In general, this project proved to be impossible.

First of all, most of the levers needed to manage the economy are in the hands of the federal government. The provinces do not control the income tax laws, interest rates, exchange rates or the money supply. They cannot touch most tax loopholes, offer cheap credit, stimulate exports by reducing the value of the dollar, or shrink the value of the debt by creating inflation. Second, the economic value of increased provincial government spending is doubtful, even in Ontario, since so much of the money leaks into other regions and other countries.

Third, the federal NDP's tax arithmetic did not add up. The Saskatchewan NDP clobbered the rich and the middle classes with new taxes and still had to impose spending cuts in order to reduce its deficit. The B.C. government imposed 26 different tax increases in its second budget, with a strong bias against upper-income earners, but also restricted spending increases on health and education to below the rate of inflation, provoking a furious backlash from organized teachers.

Historian Desmond Morton has written that everyone expected the NDP to hold a giant barbecue for its friends after its election in the provinces. Provincial public-sector workers in particular, many of them strong supporters of the NDP in the past, did not want to hear about recessions, deficits, rising health costs or public opinion.

In Ontario, a New Democratic Party with an Us-and-Them tradition in opposition suffered heartbreak in government. An inexperienced cabinet with a doubtful mandate ran into perhaps the worst economic crisis in the province's history. The government raised taxes, but also grabbed $2 billion from its own workers in a misnamed "social contract" exercise. Compared with government actions in conservative-run provinces, the Ontario measures were mild; out of 900,000 public-sector workers, 93 claimed compensation for layoff in the first nine months after the social contract became law. However, the public service unions, along with many in the social movements, saw the social contract as an unforgivable violation of union contracts.

Neither the Ontario NDP leadership nor its supporters were prepared for power. They endured shock after shock, and not just because of scandals in cabinet. They learned that deficits matter; that "the rich" include many schoolteachers and auto workers; and that corporate tax payments depend partly on profit levels. It took two years to produce guidelines for a social democratic industrial strategy, and more months before business and labour in various sectors sat down to discuss the future. The government experimented for three years before it could run an effective jobs program, even on a modest scale.

Under the leadership of Audrey McLaughlin, meanwhile, the federal NDP caucus continued on its traditional economic track, campaigning in populist style against the Goods and Services Tax and then the proposed North American Free Trade Agreement.

The grounds for the GST fight were shaky; even the researchers assigned to find alternatives to the sales tax did not believe their own arithmetic. The NDP MPs seemed, in fact, to be attacking the NDP's political base by fuelling "a tax revolt that eroded popular willingness to fund redistributive programs."[21]

The NAFTA battle was fought in the protectionist spirit of 1988, although the poorly paid Mexican working class were generally treated not as rivals but as fellow victims of corporate greed. In arguments in the Commons against NAFTA, NDP speakers called for an agreement to protect wage standards in both Canada and Mexico, but spent very little time on positive proposals for trade.

McLaughlin's communications strategist, Michael Balagus, says both these campaigns hurt the party in the polls.

> The public thought the trade deal ought to go, and so did we. They didn't like the GST, and neither did we ... But they didn't really want anybody to do anything, because they were scared to death about what might happen, especially if the NDP got involved. We never responded to that prior to the Jobs Plan. We simply jacked up the rhetoric: the caucus had a contest, "who can say the most times that we can get rid of the trade deal." For those Canadians we needed to attract, it was a scary, simplistic message.[22]

McLaughlin and Balagus became increasingly convinced that unemployment and its social costs offered better terrain for the NDP. Opinion surveys suggested that the NDP should package its views on jobs as part of an overall economic statement. In the United States, the Clinton and Perot presidential campaigns were riding to prominence on their economic plans. Balagus decided in 1992 that the NDP must also have a plan.

As a test of the jobs theme, Balagus developed a concept for a McLaughlin tour. Dennis Lewycky, an Ottawa expert on public consultations, proposed that McLaughlin forget canned speeches and show off her ability to work with real problems. He suggested that an NDP advance team go into a community facing a plant shutdown or a resource crisis, and pull together local interests for some preliminary meetings. McLaughlin could then arrive for a summit where the community could define alternatives for action.

Balagus rejected this labour-intensive approach, and settled on a TV panel-show format. Through October and November 1992, McLaughlin played host and moderator at public meetings on jobs and unemployment in Halifax, Hamilton, Winnipeg and Vancouver. At each event, a few local experts or activists discussed the regional economy. Members of the audience then commented, some with great insight, on the problems faced by local industries working in the shadow of the multinationals.

McLaughlin's meetings allowed her to say later that she had consulted with Canadians about the economy. This was not really true; nobody at the meetings took notes, and the public's ideas vanished into thin air. At the same time, they offered solid evidence that many party supporters appreciated the need for an economic plan and an industrial strategy.

The NDP developed its Jobs Plan not from public consultation, but within a strategy committee called the Policy and Issues Group, which had been formed to prepare a platform document for the coming election. In late 1992, the group was instructed by the party's Election Planning Committee to focus on jobs and the economy. Its co-chair, Dave Mackenzie from the Steelworkers, was part of a small caucus of Ontario union officials who wanted to renew social democracy in Canada. Ever since 1975 and the Liberal wage controls, labour had followed a fight-back agenda, opposed to government restraint, privatization and free trade. Some private-sector unions, ravaged by a long recession, wanted something more positive: perhaps labour could take a hand in helping to build new high-wage, high-skill opportunities. Fifteen party activists attended the group's meetings, including MPs Steven Langdon and Howard McCurdy. Mackenzie also asked numerous trade unions for ideas, although he admits he "didn't always get a lot of useful stuff."[23]

The Jobs Plan, released on February 16, 1993, proposed to create 500,000 additional jobs over five years through public works, the development of the private sector, and various taxation and interest-rate measures. It earned some applause from the mainstream media, but was rejected on balance because of its optimistic forecast about the effects of scrapping the Canada-U.S. trade deal. The Plan highlighted the party's traditional concerns for social justice and equality, but it also showed an evolution in economic thinking. It talked of "labour-management strategic alliances," an idea that had been taboo in the CLC for many years. It proposed a national development fund that would invest according to economic merit, a risqué notion for a party that had often defended ailing industries and dying resource towns. It also proposed phasing out the GST, rather than outright abolition, and offered some new ideas on international trade.

The Plan expressed deep concern about the public debt. It noted that in Sweden, the perennial model for the NDP, total government debt amounts to 3.4 per cent of the gross domestic product, compared with 53.9 per cent for Canada (in 1992). It called for the reallocation of federal spending, rather than increased spending, and it included a timetable for reducing the size of the federal deficit over time.

The Jobs Plan did not cure the NDP's economic credibility problem overnight. It did not fill every hole in NDP logic. It left aside some aspects of the economy — for example, the income gap between the rich, the middle classes and the poor. Many criticized its public works package as old-fashioned. All the same, it marked an important step for the NDP in its emphasis on innovation, brainpower, worker participation, and timely investment in growing firms and industrial clusters. Its goal was to make Canada a source of high-value goods and services for the world market, and at the same time to build links between capital and the community, including workers.

The Liberal jobs plan, released in September 1993, had more pages than the NDP plan, but covered less ground. It said nothing about tax policy or trade policy, its training scheme for industry had no teeth, it ignored the role of government research centres, and it proposed only a miniature national investment fund. However, it focused public attention on jobs, and its success suggested that Canadians still prefer activist government. "After the Liberals released their Red Book," says Dave Mackenzie, "I constantly heard the rueful refrain that they were stealing from us."[24]

For years, Canadians rejected the NDP's economic arguments, and so the party buried them. Isolated from debate and new information, the party's economic policies grew stale. In the absence of vital economic policies, the NDP's overall program became irrelevant. Instead of educating themselves and challenging their opposition, New Democrats turned their reputation for economic incompetence into their trademark.

If the NDP can muster the resources to begin again, and design up-to-date proposals for the national economy, it will have no problem finding examples and allies. The NDP provincial governments, working with organized labour and private interests, have taken various steps to generate jobs or at least prevent privately owned industries from self-destructing. And in the leading ranks of the trade unions, even in public-sector unions like the Canadian Union of Public Employees, there is a new pragmatism in seeking economic solutions.

I don't think our strategies have been tried and failed in this country. It's the strategies of the other side. The Liberals talk about getting rid of the deficit by looking at social programs. Well, we had a Tory government already ... It's only when you reduce unemployment that you boost government revenues. If we can set targets for reducing the deficit, why can't we have targets for reducing unemployment?

We're not saying government has to create all the jobs. Government's role is to work with business and labour in each sector to encourage the development of manufacturing and services ...[25]

Some have argued in the past that the NDP's links to a self-interested trade union movement have limited the party's proposals on the economy to simple Us-and-Them formulas. In the 1990s, guided partly by examples in Europe and Quebec, Canadian unions are re-examining the future of the productive economy. Unionized workers have voting power, organizing power and growing financial resources, and so do their counterparts around the northern industrial world.[26] At the same time, unions confront an international corporate culture that is increasingly indifferent to workers, communities and ecosystems. Unions, communities, provinces and nation-states face an absolute need to make industry more accountable and to look for allies of like mind in other countries. "It's a period when everything is malleable. When everything is fine, nobody wants to change anything. This is an opportunity to change ... More of the same is impossible."[27]

Several NDP-affiliated unions have started by pressing for a voice in the day-to-day operation of the workplace. Workers face real hazards in going down this road — that is, in accepting more responsibilities and liabilities while leaving ultimate power with corporate boards of directors. However, some unions such as the Steelworkers are taking the plunge, working from some of the same assumptions that shaped the Jobs Plan. Steelworkers members have started to assume some ownership of the steel industry, and some responsibility for training and product quality through a steel industry council.

Some union activists, especially in the Auto Workers, reject this trend as "old-fashioned business unionism" — that is, a sell-out of the workers by well-paid union hacks. They see co-management as a distraction from the unions' real purpose, which is to "take wages and working conditions out of competition by setting standards and defending them," as well as to set up new coalitions with citizens in the community.[28] The Steelworkers disagree, arguing that that the new partnerships with management represent "a natural extension of the basic union struggle to extend influence and control by workers over decisions they have rarely shared."[29] It is notable that the giant Public Employees union, in some respects an ally of the Auto Workers, is also venturing into wider labour-management consultation in the public sector.

At a time when the federal NDP has lost its momentum, the unions are opening a testing ground in Canada for social democratic ideas about the economy. They have rediscovered a direction that Ed Broadbent described in the late 1960s as the future of social democracy. Audrey McLaughlin expressed support in her book for this direction, suggesting tax incentives to promote worker ownership, the creation of labour-management committees to plan strategies for innovation at the plant and sectoral levels, and continued experiments with decision-making in the workplace.

"None of this will happen on a wide scale," cautions Joy Langan, the former NDP labour critic, "until we have a Canada that respects trade unions and grants them a right to exist. We don't have that now. Maybe we never will."[30] The unions that have taken the first steps are under pressure to prove the benefits to the rest of organized labour. If they succeed, they may establish a new electoral base for social democratic politics and a new public credibility for social democratic ideas; and as a result, they may help elect governments that will give unions room to breathe and flourish.[31]

There is some danger here of overstating this positive trend. The unions are small institutions, and will not radically change the behaviour of Canadian business acting by themselves. The job of building links among labour, the community and business in order to protect Canadian jobs will only be done by a social democratic government. Instead, we have at the federal level a social democratic party, or a semi–social democratic party, that lacks influence.

The federal NDP has won respect through many elections for its tireless defence of medicare and the unemployed. Its ideas for eliminating wasteful tax loopholes have proven popular, even if the benefits were overstated. But these strengths are not enough. Without a saleable plan for the management of the economy — and the management of the public sector, which is another can of worms entirely — voters will not take the NDP seriously as a party of government. The *only* place for the party to begin is to persuade past and present party supporters, the left populists and gut socialists, that an active, imaginative compromise between an ideal democracy and the market system is worth pursuing. The alternative is for the NDP to keep on complaining, in a passive, victimized tone, about "Them," about their thoughtless behaviour, their failure to support social programs, and especially their exodus to other countries and the waning of capitalist prosperity in Canada.

7

The 1993 Campaign

Only one party understands what is happening in the real world out there.

— Audrey McLaughlin[1]

Six days before the 1993 election, most of the NDP's Ottawa staff boarded the McLaughlin campaign jet for Winnipeg. The campaign directors had rerouted the plane for a special airlift to the West, leaving the leader behind in Toronto. Nineteen researchers and organizers would join phone banks and door-knocking brigades in formerly safe NDP seats. For the passengers, several months of grinding work were almost at an end. The mood aboard the flight was as euphoric as a schoolroom in June.

The party now had only one objective, to win 12 seats and keep its official status in Parliament, but the polls showed that voters were still shifting to the Liberals in order to defeat the Conservatives. The NDP strategists tried to reverse the flow. "The Tories are dead. There are no more worries about the Tories coming back, so anybody who was thinking of voting strategically ... come on home."[2]

I spent the last days in the mausoleum stillness of the campaign headquarters in Ottawa. The phones had died. Reporters, local activists and the public had stopped calling. There was little to do except compose the daily bulletin to all campaigns ("The Tories are dead. There are no more worries ...") and listen to the wind in the bare branches outside.

Ever since 1988, the NDP's election planners had worked with two cardinal rules: keep the next campaign open for consultation, and don't ignore free trade. The provincial sections wanted to prevent domination from Ottawa. Labour New Democrats were determined the party would not bungle the trade issue for a second time.

Audrey McLaughlin's advisers, Campbell and Balagus, had pitched for a campaign based on leadership politics and fighting the

Liberals. McLaughlin, they argued through 1992, was the only woman leader, she had fresh ideas, and she would express them honestly and clearly. The Liberals were the real opposition, competing for votes in the NDP universe. Confronting the Conservatives and Reform was a waste of time.

McLaughlin had taken steps to head off a repeat of 1988, in particular by giving the party's Strategic and Election Planning Committee (SEPC) more authority and more members from across Canada. However, the SEPC relied on the work of paid staff in Ottawa, and in late 1992 the senior staff began to depart, tired of politics or of the McLaughlin regime, or eased out. Federal secretary Dick Proctor left his job at headquarters, followed by the party fundraiser, the director of organizing, and the communications officer. On Parliament Hill, the leader's principal secretary resigned, followed by the research director.

The party organization found a capable new federal secretary, Fraser Green, an experienced political organizer and team leader. The change of staff in the leader's office went less smoothly. The new principal secretary, Sandra Mitchell, demanded that McLaughlin fire Michael Balagus, the communications director. The leader refused, and Mitchell and Balagus began to feud with each other. Balagus had taken on a wide range of election preparation tasks, and Mitchell told anyone who would listen that he was "way over his head ... completely incompetent ... without redeeming qualities ..."[3]

As 1993 began, MPs and SEPC members grew impatient. Somebody, they complained, should craft a unifying message, a successor to the slogan "we're standing up for ordinary Canadians," which had crystallized the party's appeal to voters in 1984. Balagus still wanted a leader-centred campaign, but he now proposed to combine it with a crusade for job creation. Others argued that the party's opposition to the North American Free Trade Agreement (NAFTA) could tie the NDP's social, economic and nationalist concerns together. Others, especially on the Prairies, regarded NAFTA as a side issue and a vote-loser. The compromise came down to a refusal to choose.

At the same time, the NDP was undecided about how to treat the other parties. New Democrats had trouble understanding how voters could take either Jean Chrétien or Preston Manning seriously. Chrétien spoke out on everything, and seemed to say nothing. Manning, the self-styled champion of democracy, was clearly a tyrant. Should the NDP attack Chrétien, or the Liberals' policies, or the Liberals' silence on policy? Or should New Democrats thump the

Tories, and prove they were better Tory-thumpers than the Liberals? Or did good New Democrats avoid negative politics?

And how long could the NDP ignore Reform?

Furthermore, the polls showed that in the eyes of the public, McLaughlin's profile remained fuzzy. Jim Ryan, a partner in the NDP's advertising agency, says "a lot of people didn't know who she was, or what she was about."[4] Sandra Mitchell says she urged the leader to "go to charm school" and improve her public presence, but McLaughlin declined. "I had not had any long conversations with her since June 1991. I found her to be quite changed. She had forgotten how to listen ... I found her to be very bitter, despondent, depressed, angry, prickly."[5]

The party had hoped to buy some TV advertising and send McLaughlin on a pre-election tour in January and February 1993, but a cash squeeze forced a delay. When the money arrived, the tour was put off because Brian Mulroney had resigned as Conservative leader, and the strategists saw no point in competing for publicity with a Tory leadership race.

In early March, Fraser Green and Michael Balagus appealed to strategists from past years to help the party find a direction. They brought together 15 senior politicos, including former Ontario leader Stephen Lewis, and Bill Knight and George Nakitsas from the 1988 campaign. To the chagrin of some, Balagus also invited the recently departed Les Campbell.

It was a rocky meeting. Balagus's two-page strategic summary moved Nakitsas to remark, "You've left out the MPs, you've left out labour, you've left out the provinces, you've left out the party, and you've left out the staff. Otherwise it's a good plan." Campbell talked about his discussions with Tory strategists and drew diagrams showing how the Conservatives and the NDP could squeeze the Liberals. Stephen Lewis's response was, "Did you know how to draw those circles before you had Tory friends?"

Later that day, Balagus and SEPC chair Julie Davis talked to Jane Taber of *The Ottawa Citizen*, who wrote a glowing column on the NDP's campaign plans. Carol Phillips, the executive assistant to CLC president Robert White and a key McLaughlin backer in 1989, read the column and wrote to Balagus in desperation. "Give me a break. We must've been at different meetings ..."

If, after our meeting and your document, I was asked to explain to anyone else what our overall campaign message was, I would be at a loss to do so. Simply continuing to repeat and repeat, as you do no less than three times in your paper, that our positive messages are 1) Audrey, 2) On your side, 3) Jobs Plan, 4) NAFTA and that our negative messages are 1) Chrétien, 2) Libs no policy, 3) Libs on NAFTA, and 4) Tory is a Tory, are more like a series of mantras than a coherent theme or strategy for campaign ...

I know you say that it is too early to finalize a campaign strategy and that we must be flexible. I don't think I agree. Surely by now certain general approaches to the campaign, certain themes, an overall strategic sense, should have been formulated.[6]

Phillips concluded that, with the Rae government's loss of support in Ontario and the federal party's low standing in the polls, it was "impossible" to exaggerate the demoralization among party members. She expressed grave worries about the coming campaign.

An SEPC discussion paper dated April 17 showed continued hesitation among the strategists. The first priority after an election call would be to establish "a credible role"; however, it was unclear whether the NDP, sitting at 12 per cent, should firm up its base vote or chase "former and soft Liberals." The paper speculated that the media and the larger parties might build the campaign around any of three issues:

1. *Deficit*: "Audrey McLaughlin and her team of working Canadians will fight to see that working Canadians are protected and that the people who benefited from the debt pay for the debt." Or, alternatively, "The only way to reduce the deficit is to get people working again."

2. *Leadership*: "Only Audrey McLaughlin and her team of working Canadians are on your side."

3. *Jobs and NAFTA*: "Only the NDP will stop the loss of jobs by cancelling the FTA and NAFTA."[7]

Finally, in June — a day or two after the Alberta New Democrats lost every one of their 15 seats in a provincial election — the SEPC decided to select a single campaign theme, and use it right up until the election. The polls rated jobs, finding them and keeping them, as the number one issue in Canada, and the media were picking up the story. The New Democrats, therefore, would campaign on job creation, an issue that Balagus had promoted for close to a year.

The slogan was, "Canada Works when Canadians Work." The NDP had a realistic, sensible plan for full employment. The federal government, working with the provinces, could help generate good, high-skill jobs. The NDP would not form the government, but it could pressure the other parties to adopt a jobs agenda.

On June 16, a sunny day in Ottawa's downtown Minto Park, McLaughlin kicked off a 15-city Canadian tour with a speech to local activists and NDP staff. Unhappily, the media lost the jobs message in the mix of references to the NDP's courageous stands on abortion, the Gulf War and free trade. Kim Campbell had emerged as the winner at the Conservative convention; McLaughlin said Canadians now had a choice between a woman who had always supported Brian Mulroney and a woman who had opposed him. (The NDP never quite knew what to do with the gender issue after Campbell's entry; on this occasion, party president Nancy Riche said it was time to stop judging people by their gender.)

The NDP would run again on the Us-and-Them motif, Geoffrey York wrote in *The Globe*; it would respond to the economic insecurity of the middle class and working class. He quoted McLaughlin as saying, "Only one party understands what's happening in the real world out there."[8]

Jobs was the theme, the theme was jobs. McLaughlin travelled to Halifax the next day and proposed to create jobs with a national child care program. It was the only tour event that captured nationwide news; every headline blared out the cost of the program: $3.75 billion. Sensible? Realistic? "Expensive and utopian," wrote a normally sympathetic reporter.[9]

On the Ontario leg of the tour, reporters ignored jobs and pressed for McLaughlin's views on the Ontario NDP. Bob Rae had tabled his "social contract" bill, and his government and the public sector unions were at war. McLaughlin ran into anti-Rae hecklers even at NDP membership meetings. She told the media she "couldn't say how she would have handled the provincial government's social contract," but saw "no need to distance herself" from the premier.[10]

The Canadian Press published the first obituary for the federal NDP. It blamed, first, the Rae government's unpopularity across Canada, and second, the fact that McLaughlin remained "an enigma" to voters.[11] Don't be cruel to the federal leader, replied the ultra-Tory

Thomson News: "Audrey McLaughlin, poor soul, deserves our admiration."[12]

The election loomed. The SEPC's working group, chaired by Julie Davis and Fraser Green and made up of a dozen party staff and senior labour staff, met more often. Tension swirled around Michael Balagus. Most of the group were Ontario-based; Balagus told them to forget about Ontario, that Canada's largest province was lost. Some felt Balagus was defying group decisions. The SEPC approved a magazine ad featuring McLaughlin; Balagus scheduled a Wednesday morning unveiling; he then postponed it, permanently as it turned out, because McLaughlin wanted to do her laundry. The working group wanted the NDP to launch its new report on the deficit with some fanfare; Balagus insisted the leader must release the report at a news conference; after a delay, he reported that McLaughlin had rejected the idea. The diplomatic Green expressed a private wish to break Balagus's nose.

Provincial NDP notables complained that McLaughlin refused to meet with the premiers, and they blamed Balagus. She had gone to Saskatchewan without seeing Romanow. She had practically walked past Bob Rae at a union convention. Balagus argued that this pre-election period should be McLaughlin's time; she must make her own news and escape the shadow of male premiers.

At federal headquarters, the cash dried up. The party had a record number of organizers on the payroll, but the fundraising letters barely paid for themselves. In the communications office, I paid for paper and postage from my own pocket, and raised money from my friends. Down the hall, my colleagues sat hunched over the phones, patiently trying to persuade New Democrats to stand as candidates in Ontario and the Atlantic region. The new affirmative action guidelines gave white men, women, and people from visible minority groups an equal opportunity to decline the job.

McLaughlin decided to boost party morale by sending a letter to federal candidates and executive members. Instead of assigning the job to an assistant, she took the rare step of drafting three pages on her home computer. She wrote that she had loved her cross-Canada tour, and expressed doubts about polls that put the NDP at 8 per cent of the decided vote.

I wish that all of you could have been on that pre-election tour. I found the experience energizing, invigorating — to see the quality and enthusiasm of our candidates, the support for our

incumbents, and the real faith in us. And the further I got from
Ottawa, I found that people were not fazed by polls, not cynical,
and truly believing we can make a difference ...

As one who has the privilege to meet people from all across
the country in all walks of life, I am convinced that no one
expects that a political party or leader has all the answers. But
there is a place for a party that gives voice to those who have
not been heard.[13]

A few days after submitting this draft to Green for editing and
distribution, McLaughlin offered to resign.

The offer came at an special executive meeting called to discuss
the crisis in Ontario. Up to this point, McLaughlin had refused to
criticize Bob Rae, but Ontario labour leaders — including Julie
Davis, the co-chair of the federal campaign — wanted a clear federal
position on the Ontario social contract. On a sweltering July day, the
federal executive gathered in a hotel basement, the dank bottom of
a 19-storey column of overchilled air.

First into the hall were the table officers — the president, vice-
presidents, treasurer and secretary. Everyone else was barred, except
a pollster who burst in to retrieve a suitcase. McLaughlin spoke
briefly. If the party wanted her resignation, she would resign, although she would prefer to stay. The group responded with a quiet,
firm refusal. It was a small meeting, but within hours word had
leaked to the media, and the pundits were saying that her leadership
had been further weakened.

The broader executive debated a statement upholding the principle
of collective bargaining. While the delegates shivered and spoke in
turn, the leader sighed and wrote notes to herself. The diplomatically
worded statement aimed an implied criticism at the Rae government's social contract. It got minimal press attention, but New
Democrats made note of it: Buzz Hargrove, president of the Auto
Workers, called it a new beginning, while party members on the
Prairies complained of a public sell-out to Ontario labour.

The Election Planning working group hatched a final pre-election
scheme. Fraser Green would spend the last financial reserves on an
August television campaign. It would feature a televised town hall
meeting, Bill Clinton style, and some ads where McLaughlin would
explain why she had entered politics.

Preparations for the town hall, booked on Ontario's Global TV
network for August 11, proceeded by hiccups. Headquarters staff

blamed Balagus's habit of carrying everything in his head. They sent invitations to dozens of lobby groups and individuals, and then got word that the party could not afford the $40,000 cost. They made calls to cancel the invitations, only to learn the show was on again.

Balagus had agreed in early July to oversee production of a short Audrey McLaughlin video to open the town hall show. On Thursday, August 5, six days before the event, Green asked me to search my office for any historic footage and send it over to Balagus on the Hill. I wondered what the hell was going on.

As it turned out, the program from Toronto went smoothly. McLaughlin sailed through the questions from the studio audience. The video, focusing on her ties to regular folks, was well received. The news reporters, however, noted that it bore a "Made in U.S.A." label. Balagus admitted the video had been produced in a hurry; he said the final edit had been done in Washington, D.C., because no Canadian production house was available for a rush job. The Canadian video production industry cried out in protest. Editorial writers revelled at the anti–free trade party's hypocrisy, "the bishop caught in the brothel, the prohibition zealot found in a gin mill ..."[14]

McLaughlin, trying to protect her man, was "very proud of the video that was done, and pleased that it's been produced and Canadians get to see me in a different light."[15] But the story was too big to contain. In terms of the volume of inquiries from the media, it was probably the biggest NDP news story of the year. The heat on the SEPC from party members grew intense. The $50,000 video was now junk. On Tuesday, August 17, three weeks before the election call, Balagus resigned. Some say he had only carried out a group decision to send the video to Washington, some say he acted alone. In any case, his time had come.

By the end of the day, Roy Romanow had assigned his top aide to fill in as communications director for the federal campaign. Garry Aldridge reached Ottawa in time to get his bearings and draft an opening statement for McLaughlin.

Using Romanow's move as a precedent, the federal headquarters persuaded Premier Rae to give up his administrative head, Richard McLelland, to act as the leader's tour director. McLelland tore apart almost everything Balagus had left.

Green and Julie Davis also prevailed on Julie Mason, who had worked on the NDP TV ads in 1988, to take over Balagus's work with the advertising agency in producing ads and booking time. In summary, then, the SEPC needed at least three high-level professionals to do the work that Balagus had undertaken.

Balagus had got himself impossibly overextended, to the detriment of the 1993 campaign. He was bright, creative and hungry to take on important tasks, and the other strategists had let him go ahead. There had been some grumbling, and then mounting fear that planning for the tour was far behind schedule; SEPC working group member Michael Lewis says Balagus's departure "should have happened sooner."[16] But remembering the conflict of 1988, the NDP team had developed a passive working style geared as much to avoiding trouble as to getting the job done. Among other things, they had not wanted to confront McLaughlin about Balagus, knowing that she would fight tenaciously to protect him.

McLaughlin read Garry Aldridge's opening statement at the National Press Theatre on September 6, a few hours after the election date was announced. It combined the rhetoric of "Us and Them" with a list of issues, jobs at the top.

"This election is about jobs and the economy and real change," she said. "Canadians are asking: who can I count on to fight for me and my interests?"

"Jean Chrétien promises change, but can you really count on him?" McLaughlin dismissed Chrétien's claims to oppose NAFTA and patronage, and his promise to change the GST. "On issue after issue, you just can't count on Jean Chrétien."

"Every New Democrat you elect will be one more vote, one more voice, to make jobs Canada's number one priority; one more vote, one more voice, to fight NAFTA; to speak out for fair taxation; and to protect medicare."[17]

A thousand words and it was done. McLaughlin was off to see the country. The Langdon affair, her offer to resign and the Balagus fiasco were behind her. Over the next seven weeks, she was assertive and consistent, and her confidence grew visibly. At her side she had the support team she had always deserved, in the formidable trio of Tessa Hebb, the new research director, Sharon Vance from Montreal and Laura Nichols from British Columbia. Her tour would be more gently paced than Broadbent's in 1988, and her entourage more disciplined. In the leaders' debate, traditionally the do-or-die moment for party leaders, her presence and tenacity surprised many viewers. Unhappily, the polls confirmed that she was not winning votes for the NDP.

The NDP, praying for voter volatility, started the campaign at 8 per cent, peaked at 10 in the second week, and trailed off to 7. Only 4 per cent of Canadians wanted to see Audrey McLaughlin become prime minister, compared with 3 per cent for Mel Hurtig of the upstart National Party. The NDP's miraculously full slate of candidates included 110 women, a Canadian record, but this achievement generated hardly a ripple. The tour introduced some "new politics," in the form of McLaughlin meeting at round tables with ordinary folks, but the media ignored it. Instead, they wrote portraits of the leader's dignity among the ruins.

The campaign directors, polling 75 ridings, searched in vain for signs of interest in the NDP. In our daily bulletins and sample flyers, the communications group presented arguments on jobs, medicare, the drug patent sell-out, trade and Liberal patronage. One by one, Green and Aldridge weeded the arguments out. The first phrase to go was "real change." Voters, for some reason, seemed to associate change with the Liberals and Reform.

At the end of a discouraging first week, campaign directors Green and Davis had to choose a tone and a theme for a first round of television advertisements. (Under the election law, the parties could advertise only in the final 28 days of the campaign.) The NDP would spend its advertising budget almost entirely on television, mostly in the West, and almost entirely in English. Working with Ryan Macdonald Edwards of Toronto, the strategists decided that the tone would be one of rage. The theme was "Us and Them," expressed here as "Ottawa Doesn't Get the Message. Send It," echoing the "Send them a message" slogans that had helped elect Bob Rae in Ontario.

The NDP had set its 1988 ads in the colour-coordinated world of most TV commercials. The 1993 ads, black and white, gritty, over-exposed, featured "ordinary Canadians" shouting in anger about medicare, jobs, helicopters and political patronage. Green explained to a media briefing that voters were fed up with Ottawa acting for big interests and political parties, and they wanted someone to speak up for their interests.

Ryan Macdonald Edwards designed the ads to get viewers to take notice. The NDP was declaring "We're still here!" However, says Jim Ryan, "I think we went into this thing with the wrong set of explanations — the wrong stands, policies, stridency. It just doesn't work any more. I disagree with the idea of ordinary Canadians. If you are ordinary, you don't want to be. We all aspire to more than we have." [18]

After months of promising a positive campaign, the NDP had fallen back on a negative approach that showed working people as victims. Instead of offering hope for collective action, the ads played on fear and individual alienation. The experts on the media panels said they would drive voters to Reform. After two weeks, the campaign directors ordered new ads — first, a segment with McLaughlin discussing medicare, later a morbid black-and-white scare piece on the death of medicare. The B.C. NDP, unhappy with the federal product, produced their own anti-Liberal and anti-Reform ads.

"The messaging changed," says Jim Ryan, "but the momentum was with the other parties."

From a desk in federal headquarters, Michael Lewis chatted every day with senior labour leaders. They agreed, reluctantly, that the NAFTA issue had not caught the public imagination, despite their earlier enthusiasm for it. NAFTA was demoted to marginal status in McLaughlin's speeches and the sample "literature" we sent out to the local campaigns from Ottawa.

The next casualty was the jobs issue. When Jean Chrétien unveiled his Red Book on job creation, he eclipsed the 60-page policy statement McLaughlin had released in February. New Democrat researchers argued that the Liberals' logic was full of holes; unfortunately, their book was more expensively designed and easier to read. The NDP, overwhelmed by the Liberals' superior reputation for economic management, backed away from a duel over the two documents. NDP headquarters continued to ship out 16-page summaries of the Jobs Plan — more than a million went to local campaigns — but the promise to push for jobs was dropped from McLaughlin's speeches.

"It had been my hope that by trying to become more sophisticated, by talking about new high-tech strategies, that the Jobs Plan would give us some credibility," says Dave Mackenzie, one of the Plan's architects. "But we were fighting three decades of the party's history. I just hope we don't go back to ignoring the employment creation and wealth creation side of life."[19]

Political scientist Daniel Drache says the Liberal plan indicated a shift in that party's identity, a new willingness to offer substance. The Liberals were happy to play on NDP turf, and they would take political risks to get there. Drache says voters did not see the New Democrat plan as an advance in either substance or process. And for the voters, says Drache, "What's the difference between a courageous left-Liberal and a non-courageous New Democrat? Nothing!"[20]

With the effective shelving of the NDP Jobs Plan, the campaign lost its only link to issues of economic management or wealth creation. From here on, Canadian enterprise existed only as a punching bag, in the form of "the rich and the powerful" and "corporate lobbyists."

The attacks on the corporate bad guys took on a special piquance for me when I started listing corporate donations to the Liberals and Reform in the daily bulletin. After a couple of days I had second thoughts and requested a report on corporate contributions to the NDP. The record for 1991 showed, among many others, a $2,250 donation from Extendicare Health Services; $5,110.55 from the Ontario Medical Association; and by a strange twist, $3,850 from Lang Michener Management, a corporate cousin of Jean Chrétien's old law firm. In all, the file for one year showed 57 corporate donations in amounts of $2,000 or more.[21] How long could the NDP go on pretending that these institutions were the enemy?

By the mid-way point, the central campaign had narrowed its focus to the following: we're on your side, save medicare, tax the rich, don't trust the Liberals. In her brief opening statement in the English leaders' debate, McLaughlin touched on all these themes. "Ottawa should go after the rich who've been getting a free ride in this country, and leave your Medicare alone!"[22]

The National Action Committee on the Status of Women, aboriginals and minority groups complained that the NDP had pushed their concerns aside. McLaughlin's years of work in the Commons and across the country did not count. At the same time, many in the white male-stream felt the party was ignoring them, too. "We were not seen as representing 'people like us' — that is, the blue collar workers," says defeated MP John Brewin.[23] Dawn Black, the firebrand of women's politics in Parliament, says the same complaint contributed to her loss to Reform in New Westminster. "Some of our traditional support felt a little bit antsy about a perception that we were only speaking to narrow interest groups and not to the community as a whole."[24]

The origins of this feeling — that the NDP had abandoned average families — are hard to trace. Perhaps they originated in the referendum, the NDP's affirmative action policies, the lack of gut populist appeal among NDP leaders, or the slow evolution of the party from a workers' movement into a bureaucratic machine. Or perhaps it was the families who had changed, and the NDP that had stood still.

The best-known figures in the federal NDP were fighting for their political lives, and most were losing. They knew their ridings well, they had the experience to adapt the party message to local conditions, and they had seasoned organizers behind them, but long-time supporters were turning away.

In Esquimalt, voters chided populist crusader Dave Barrett for drawing a former premier's pension while serving as an MP. They complained about the use of public money in the previous year's Yes campaign, the unfair treatment of newer parties in the awarding of election advertising time, and the perception that politicians "just didn't listen." His campaign chair says Barrett forgot about federal headquarters and ran on the message "Dave, Dave, Dave will fight for you."[25] By questioning the Reform Party's plans for old-age pensions and medicare, Barrett recovered some former support, but it wasn't enough.

In Nickel Belt, MP John Rodriguez ignored the party and talked about his record of bringing federal money to the riding. He won the backing of the local paper and a historic common front of local unions, and got half the votes of his Liberal rival.

In Ottawa Centre, former MP Marion Dewar campaigned on her own issues and image. If any candidate could swing a riding, it should have been Dewar; the distinguished ex-mayor had a record of drawing support from all parties. She lost badly to a Liberal whose own party considered him a liability.

Chris Axworthy, with hundreds of volunteers, almost lost Saskatoon–Clark's Crossing to a Reform candidate campaigning alone.

> People had given up listening to us a long time before. So when we talked about saving medicare, nobody listened to us. Plus they didn't think medicare was under any threat, anyway ...
>
> Somebody phoned me during the election, and said, "Look, I'm not an aboriginal person, I'm not on welfare, and I'm not disabled. You're not speaking to me." ... Besides, people who were aboriginals didn't vote as aboriginals, people who were gay didn't vote as gays. They voted looking for some hope in the economy. It didn't matter that we had stood up for them every time on "their issue." Our marketing was way off.

If you asked most MPs and they were honest, they would have said, "I don't know what we stand for. We're in favour of fairness and all that, but what does that mean?"

The world was changing and we were not. People had a sense that they couldn't hang on to the things we wanted to hang on to ... We became a very conservative party in a changing world.[26]

"We were living off the credit built up by Tommy Douglas and Stanley Knowles," says defeated MP Ian Waddell.[27] "We were always defending the status quo," says John Brewin, "health care and the social service network and things we had fought for over the years. We were *against* free trade, *against* NAFTA, but we didn't know where we wanted to go."[28]

The provincial government factor also hurt the federal NDP. It was worst in Ontario, significant in British Columbia, less significant in Saskatchewan. After asking McLaughlin to tiptoe around during their election campaigns, the governments operated business as usual during the federal campaign. Saskatchewan closed hospitals, while the Ontario government floated the idea of cutting social assistance to children. Defenders of the governments point out that they all remained more popular than the federal party. This is true, but there remained a widening gap between what the NDP had always said in federal opposition and what it was doing in government.

Doug Coupar, the Ottawa-based director of the national firefighters' union and a CLC activist, says dislike of the Rae government moved thousands of union militants to reduce their gifts of time and money to the federal party. In many workplaces, the "sheer hatred" for the Ontario government made it difficult for party members to campaign for the NDP.[29] The Steelworkers' Michael Lewis, a key federal strategist and the son of David Lewis, wrote a fundraising letter confessing that the Rae government's actions had brought him to "a crisis of faith." However, he cautioned against "trying to punish the government by hurting the party ... The party is us, it's our family."[30] Ontario voters punished the party; in a province with an NDP government, the federal NDP got less than 6 per cent of the vote.

There were still scattered complaints that the headquarters in Ottawa was failing to consult or listen to ideas. It was clear, though, that nobody had a magic wand. After spending a month on the phone with bewildered labour leaders, Michael Lewis went home to

Toronto well before voting day. The Action Canada Network, which had distributed a crucial anti–free trade comic in 1988, could not overcome internal problems to produce a similar piece about NAFTA. ACN chair Tony Clarke says nobody on the left had a credible position on NAFTA, or how to make it fit with the federal deficit, which had become a favourite Tory/Reform theme.[31] The anti–free trade Council of Canadians, after years of sitting on the fence between the NDP and the Liberals, endorsed a number of incumbent NDP MPs, but with no visible effect.

From the middle of a five-way struggle among parties, I had to conclude that the NDP campaign was influencing the overall election race. Unfortunately, the benefit went mostly to the Liberals. The NDP talked about jobs, and the Liberals made jobs their ticket. The NDP talked about the Conservative give-away of Pearson Airport in Toronto, and the Liberals promised to reverse the decision. The NDP pointed out the far-right tendencies in the Reform Party, and voters fled to the Liberals for safety.

And still the Reform tide rose. Preston Manning attracted the far right, but he also represented a new politics and what many took to be a new honesty. McLaughlin had worked to communicate her new politics since 1989, but it had not been noticed, or not believed. To the guys at the gas station in Mission, the NDP was just another establishment party.

After the leaders' debates, the NDP central campaign gave up hope for Ontario and much of British Columbia. The directors adopted the "Whatever It Takes" strategy, intended to safeguard the NDP's official status in Parliament, and narrowed the campaign focus to just 22 seats. It allowed the cash-starved party to cut spending on polling and TV ads. Most of the workers in the leader's tour and the research office joined the airlift west to help the chosen candidates; those who remained in Ottawa were to bend their efforts to the same 22 seats.

And finally, after weeks of searching for a useful argument, the campaign directors came across an apparent winner in one of the nightly polls. It read:

Imagine for a moment that Jean Chrétien and the Liberals win a majority government in this election. Would you prefer that your next Member of Parliament be a Liberal, who would influence the new government from the inside; OR a New Democrat, who would pressure the Liberals to keep their promises on job creation and health care; OR a Reformer, who would pressure the Liberals to reduce the deficit?

The question pointed voters to the conclusion that under a Liberal majority government, New Democrat MPs would speak more effectively for local interests than backbench Liberals. In the 22 ridings, 40 per cent of those surveyed by telephone agreed. Forty per cent! In a multi-party race, this would take a candidate over the top.

All the NDP had to do now was to persuade voters that there was, indeed, a Liberal majority government in the works. "THE TORIES ARE DEAD! THERE ARE NO MORE WORRIES ABOUT THE TORIES COMING BACK ..." The effort failed. Canadians on the left half of the political spectrum were determined to finish off the Tory beast, and they massed behind the Liberals. Besides, the Liberals promised jobs and medicare, just like the NDP.

On election night, most candidates accepted defeat with grace. Green had faxed out a page of notes beforehand, asking New Democrats not to blame the voters or the media. The defeated Steven Langdon blamed Bob Rae, and called on him to resign. CLC president Robert White seemed almost pleased: Canadians, it seemed, had defeated the Tory agenda. McLaughlin, appearing at midnight Eastern Time, talked exclusively to her Yukon supporters, thanking them for her own wonderful re-election until CBC cut to something else.

There would be no official status. The NDP was a rump in Parliament. Besides McLaughlin, it had elected one member from Manitoba, two from British Columbia, and five from Saskatchewan, all of them men. The social democrats could prepare for renewal or a final slide to oblivion.

8

A Better Umbrella

What the hell do New Democrats join for? So they can elect a government that can't do anything? If they don't have the support of a mass movement, they can't do anything.

— Peter Bleyer[1]

The federal NDP's defeat does not reflect a decline in social action at the grass roots. Every region of Canada has a flourishing culture of local organizations, issue groups and coalitions. At the national level the coalitions are frail, consisting of a handful of staff workers. At the base, the individual groups count millions of people. Their values often overlap with those of the NDP, but it seems many of them vote for other parties.

Even so, the NDP is sometimes criticized as a committee of interest groups. There is some truth to this. As a party of the Opposition, the NDP has often spoken up for causes and communities. As a party of the left, it has attracted large numbers of activists and staff workers from lobby groups and social agencies. But the NDP's official ties with social action movements are non-existent and with visible minority groups there are few ties of any kind. The party die-hards, the people who grew up in the party, are willing to accept the social activists individually; however, they dispute the political credentials of the social action movements. They argue that an anti-racism council, a seniors' network, a gay newspaper, or a campaign to save trees can never do the work of a party in Parliament on behalf of working people and the poor. With the crowning insult, they add that such groups are full of Liberals; and a Liberal, in NDP eyes, is an opportunist who chooses to defend the supremacy and privileges of corporate fat cats.

Robert White, the most powerful figure in organized labour in English Canada, has welcomed the growth of the social action movements. At least as far back as 1989, he urged the NDP to "identify and work with this constituency for change" and "to articulate the concerns and frustrations of working people, women fighting for equality, farmers, the poor, native people, environmentalists, and the peace movement."[2] When White's Canadian Auto Workers (CAW) split with the Rae government in Ontario, it shifted resources away from the NDP and towards coalitions of action groups. In 1993, White masterminded one of the largest political rallies in Canadian history, partly in order to introduce coalition leaders to a labour crowd.

White and other prominent trade unionists have realized that the nature of political action in Canada has changed. Community-based and issue-based organizations are now important political players in their own right, and the unions are trying to persuade them to work out relationships of mutual support. Can the NDP join this emerging common front? Can it afford not to?

David Lewis and Stanley Knowles built the New Democratic Party with the aid of the largest mass movement of the day, the labour movement. The party's first organizing committee had 20 members, 10 from the CCF and 10 from the Canadian Labour Congress (CLC).[3] The structure they put into place remains almost unchanged. Union head offices can endorse the party and donate money, but under the party constitution, only union locals can formally join.

By 1987, the party was affiliated with 692 locals representing 276,128 workers, about 13 per cent of the total strength of the CLC. Three-quarters of these workers lived in Ontario. More than half came from either the Auto Workers or the Steelworkers. Donations to the federal NDP from union locals, head offices and federations came to $1,345,000, or 19.7 per cent of total party receipts.[4] Non-CLC unions representing teachers, nurses and most contruction workers had no official ties and virtually no financial ties with the NDP.

Labour support has helped the NDP stay afloat, but it has remained below potential. All the same, there is some justice in the common definition of the NDP as a party founded to protect the position of union members. The NDP and CLC have worked together against wage controls, spending restraints on social programs, and free trade. Senior CLC officials have attended the caucus and executive meetings that shaped the party. Robert White, for example, served as both a vice-president of the NDP and chair of the CLC's Political Action Committee in the planning process that led up to the 1988 election. When White wrote his stinging public analysis of the campaign and the NDP's poor showing on the free trade issue, many New Democrats wondered how he could deny responsibility for the party's choice of strategies.

White's open letters charged that organized labour (speaking on behalf of "the working class") no longer had a voice in the affairs of its own party. He wrote that Ed Broadbent and his clique of advisers welcomed union money and organizers, but ignored labour issues when the TV crews arrived. He warned of a short-sighted and dangerous opportunism in the NDP. "Are we going to be a party that tries to finesse our way through, with the thought that we will be a serious contender for the government of Canada, or are we going to be a party that clearly knows the importance of recognizing working people ..."[5]

"It is ironic that at a time when the unions' relations with all kinds of groups outside the mainstream labour movement have overcome tensions and moved — unevenly — towards common goals, there remain sections of the NDP that still discuss the party's relationship with the working class in whispered anxieties."[6]

White is an imposing figure and not accustomed to losing. As head of the Auto Workers in Canada, he often fought the big auto makers to a draw when his American counterparts could not. He led his union's breakaway from its American parent body. He raided another CLC/NDP union, the Washington-based United Food and Commercial Workers, and brought more than 20,000 members into the CAW. White is a socialist, an advocate of class politics. Judging by his writings and those of the CAW research department, he believes that an elected socialist government, built on the rock of active, informed popular support, could do what his union has done at General Motors: call the capitalist bluff, protect wages and save jobs.

White told the NDP after the 1988 election "that the name of the game is not just to build electoral success"; an election win without a solid mandate for radical change would be meaningless. To create this mandate, he wrote, the party must promote "political mobilization at all levels" and spark a mass movement for social change with the issue groups and coalitions.[7]

In the 1989 party leadership race, Audrey McLaughlin spoke repeatedly about the need to form new connections between the NDP and other groups. She won White's endorsement, but she failed to deliver on her promises. Labour representatives sat on every party committee, and trade unionist Nancy Riche became party president, but White withdrew from the NDP executive. In 1992 he took over the presidency of the Canadian Labour Congress, which functions as a lobbying and research centre for labour outside Quebec. The anti-NDP socialist press predicted great things. "If there ever was a leader with the qualities and experience to transform the CLC into a truly dynamic central labour body it is Bob White."[8] "He's expected to electrify the movement, pushing the CLC to become a much more potent force, in a loose partnership with a broad network of social action groups."[9]

The community action movements and the labour–social action coalitions have grown up in a period when Canadians mistrust political parties and doubt their importance to society. Political scientists discuss the "decline-of-party thesis," while sociologists debate New Social Movement Theory.[10] In a 1991 survey of more than 1,800 Canadians, 81 per cent agreed that parties are "more interested in winning elections than governing afterwards." Sixty-three per cent agreed that parties "don't offer voters real choices because their policies are all pretty much the same," while 26 per cent disagreed. Most of those polled rejected the idea that parties do "a good job" of encouraging people to become active in politics.[11]

The motive for joining action groups is clear. Their volunteers can focus on the issue of their choice, deal face-to-face with decision-makers, and get concrete results, rather than "joining some stupid party, stuffing envelopes, chanting 'Bri-an, Bri-an' or 'Turn-er, Turn-er' at a 'leadership' convention, and yearning for an election victory in the hope of being appointed to some board."[12] Many people find that compared with political parties, action groups are more accessible and more democratic.

The CLC and its affiliated unions began working with other lobby groups and church-based coalitions in the 1970s, pressuring government and educating the public on poverty issues and international affairs. Labour had money and experience; the social action groups had people, ideas and a fresh credibility. There were agonizing stresses and fractures between the two sides; labour's sellout of the B.C. Solidarity coalition in the anti-Socred uprising of 1983 created long term barriers to coalition work in that province. However, in 1987, the CLC, the Council of Canadians and others formed a permanent umbrella called the Pro-Canada Network, later the Action Canada Network (ACN). It played a high-profile part in the battle against the U.S.-Canada trade deal, and later, briefly, against the Goods and Services Tax.

By working in the coalitions, labour hoped to gain a media profile apart from strikes and lockouts. The unions also hoped to win new allies — in the churches, among single mothers, artists, seniors and most important of all, among their own members. Industries and workplaces had fractured into smaller and smaller units; with the rise of part-time and short-term work, and the new self-identification of women, gays and members of minorities, the unions' claim to represent working people in all aspects of their lives had become "increasingly hollow."[13] "Workers are not just 'workers,'" Robert White wrote in 1992. "They live in communities, are concerned about their environment, disarmament, what happens to Canadian culture, the constitution. So coalitions with 'non-labour' groups may sometimes really be an expression of these other dimensions of workers' lives." In addition, White wanted to reach unorganized workers through the coalitions, "to overcome a division in the working class that we absolutely need to overcome."[14] The coalitions — the environmental networks, peace networks, the National Action Committee on the Status of Women (NAC), the Canadian Health Coalition, Action Canada — offered labour and other interests a "reality test," a Canada in microcosm, a chance to open themselves to new views and new processes.[15]

Judy Darcy, national president of the Canadian Union of Public Employees (CUPE), says her public-sector union works in coalitions in order to gain public support. "We have welfare workers building support from welfare rights groups, child care workers and home care workers doing the same. We're trying to make this a part of daily life as a CUPE activist ... It's not the same thing as political party building, though. I think it's a complement to it."[16]

Local action groups have grown roots in many Canadian cities. They provide services to the community, talking heads for the media, appointees to boards, briefings and research for government officials, and a permanent launch site for urgent issue campaigns. Many theorists suggest that these groups are part of a "backyard revolution," a realignment of civil power in all Western industrial societies.[17] On the one hand, legislatures are putting more and more responsibility in the hands of advisory councils and public agencies; on the other hand, citizens based in the social action community are giving a new political edge to formerly élite bodies such as police commissions and colleges of physicians. For the first time in many cases, people from the neighbourhood lobbies, the self-help groups and the unions are confronting the establishment and their experts.

The action groups have helped to create a new social climate that is indeed, in a modest sense, revolutionary. By confirming people in their identities as citizens, women, gays and members of minorities, and then offering leadership opportunities, they open the way for the transformation of the individual. However, does all this self-improvement lead in what Robert White or Audrey McLaughlin would call a progressive direction?

Some coalition-builders say yes: the new movements, working together, will give a new voice to the masses and build a unified alternative to the corporate vision. Other observers, including sociologists who study the groups, predict that individual groups will continue to work for multiple and often conflicting objectives, and that the work of broad coalitions will be limited to occasional protest campaigns.

The National Action Committee on the Status of Women provides an example of a stable, durable coalition with a mainstream base and a left-of-centre leadership. It has a clear, specific goal: to win legal, social and economic equality for women. NAC includes many dozens of local women's centres, women's health groups and abortion rights groups. It also takes in regional and national bodies, including labour federations, the Federation of Business and Professional Women's Groups, the Federation of Junior Leagues, and the Anglican Church. Together, NAC's 600 organizations claim more than 4 million women members, rich and poor, conservative and liberal, radical and mainstream. They make up a "parliament of women ... Certainly, no future Canadian politician, male or female, will fail to understand that rape, wife beating, abortion, pornography, sexual orientation and child care are political issues. In that, NAC and its member organizations have experienced a stunning success ..."[18]

Judy Rebick, NAC's former chair, says NAC can never endorse any political party, but it can influence public opinion on social issues and "create a political space" for the New Democratic Party.[19] Can the NDP occupy this space free of charge, or must it pay a price? Judging by NAC's behaviour in the 1993 federal campaign, the organization will only speak kindly of parties that make women's equality the centrepiece of their political agenda.

The Action Canada Network, a contrasting example, appears to have become a broad coalition in search of a focus. Founded as a vehicle for protecting Canadian jobs, culture and social programs, its organizations claim the support, in one form or another, of 15 million people. This is an impressive number, except that the largest building blocks are other coalitions such as CLC, the Confédération des syndicats nationaux, NAC, the Canadian Peace Alliance, and the Canadian Federation of Students, most of which are built on still other coalitions.

Tony Clarke, the former chair of Action Canada, would like to see the organization become a forum where national organizations can set common priorities. However, its prospects are questionable, despite its high-flying start in the 1988 anti–free trade campaign. Its internal weaknesses sidelined it during the 1993 election campaign. Clarke says that with only three or four staff, the coalition lacks "institutional muscle," and he has called on member groups to commit more money and more trained organizers. "We can't put the emphasis totally on the labour movement. We need good coalition organizers, people with a sense of how to bring sectors together. How's that going to happen?"

"A coalition is a collection of groups working on an issue," protests a coalition staff member. "It is not a force to be mobilized. And the only campaign it can do has to come from the bottom up." If this is true, Action Canada can offer only a very limited picture of what its member groups want; and the NDP will have to keep juggling the individual claims of labour bodies, seniors' organizations, the women's movement, aboriginal leaders, artists, greens, international aid groups, farmers, students and anti-poverty groups, all of whom clamour for top billing at election time. Clarke admits this is a problem. "The party that tries to broker its way around single-issue groups — that's just not the way to go in the future. It'll drive itself crazy trying to broker its way among different groups and interests."[20]

In the past, the federal NDP has offered heartfelt support to many single-issue groups within the walls of Parliament. Most MPs, says Chris Axworthy, have agreed to every demand of every group in their home riding or their critic area, within the limits of the party's Us-and-Them ideology. The farm critic demands more for farmers, the seniors' critic more for seniors, etc.[21] As in the old social gospel hymn, "all that could passed through that Gate, and no one was denied."

Broadbent, McLaughlin and other MPs have also met regularly with Tony Clarke and his colleagues. However, when it comes to the national campaigns run by labour and Action Canada, the NDP finds that its flag is not welcome at coalition events. Some social activists expect the NDP to mount parallel campaigns; Clarke mentions the party's failure to carve out a profile in the 1990 campaign against the Goods and Services Tax. "If people were asked who was opposing the tax, at least in the Western provinces, more people would have said Reform."[22] The idea of parallel campaigns offends New Democrat partisans. Hasn't the NDP paid its dues as an ally? Why should it be excluded from campaigns?

In the months leading up to the 1993 election, the NDP's attitude to the action groups soured. New Democrats resented the groups' hostility to NDP provincial governments and their refusal to criticize the federal Liberals, despite the Liberals' growing support for free trade and their other similarities to the Conservatives. The provincial secretary of a major NDP section spat out his views in memo form. "Single issue groups. One. Never come through for us. Two. Their agenda is not our agenda. Three. As soon as we come to power, they piss all over us. They don't have any broader perspective than their own single issue."

Many developments contributed to this feeling in the besieged NDP. Three vivid examples were the NDP's rupture with environmental groups in British Columbia, the federal party's worsening relations with NAC, and Bob White's 1993 rally with the coalitions in Ottawa. In British Columbia, despite the Harcourt government's good environmental record, environmental groups declared war over the decision to permit commercial logging at Clayoquot Sound. The ensuing dispute was a perfect illustration, says former MP John Brewin, of how New Democrats underestimate the social movements. The NDP government thought the controversy "would die of its own accord," says Brewin. When it didn't, "they allowed the response to be driven by the hardliners in the forest industry and the crown counsel's office."[23] Before it was over, the government had been typecast as environmental villains by the world media.

The federal party's alienation from NAC wounded many feminists in the NDP. In 1992, the women's movement and the party found themselves on opposite sides of the referendum campaign. Some NAC spokespeople warned openly that voters would punish the NDP for supporting the Charlottetown Accord, while NAC chair Judy Rebick was personally offended by Audrey McLaughlin's comments about Rebick's stand. Still, everyone knew that NDP women's critic Dawn Black maintained an excellent reputation at NAC; Rebick says it was "the best relationship we ever had with a member of Parliament." New Democrats were horrified, then, when the new NAC chair, Sunera Thobani, declared during the 1993 election campaign that the NDP had ignored the concerns of women just like the Liberals and Conservatives.

NAC had long believed, in fact, that the NDP was missing an opportunity — and letting women down — by not making women's issues the focus of Audrey McLaughlin's political strategy. "The NDP gets sucked into operating like the other parties," Rebick said later. "It doesn't look at its own constituency. The NDP knows there is a gender gap, but it doesn't play to it tactically. And they write NAC off just like the Liberals and Conservatives do."[24]

In May 1993, Robert White and the CLC hosted a giant "Reclaiming Our Future" demonstration on Parliament Hill. The CLC budgeted $120,000 for the event, and CLC unions spent several times that amount chartering trains and an estimated 700 buses for their members. White told the crowd of more than 60,000 that politicians were not on the side of working people, and he made no exceptions. Tony Clarke, Judy Rebick, Ron George of the Native Council and diverse labour leaders also spoke; some shot darts at the Conservatives, some at Bob Rae, but nobody mentioned Liberals. McLaughlin hovered about the stage, but White, who had promised the coalitions a "non-partisan" afternoon, did not invite her to the microphone.

This splendid, lavish, useless event resulted in nothing, but it signalled very serious trouble for the NDP, once the party of labour. By promoting the view that all politicians were the same, and by attacking the Conservative record at the same time, the speakers effectively invited the audience to vote Liberal wherever Liberals were likely to win.

New Democrats like Joy Langan, a former labour official and member of Parliament, concluded that the time spent by committed New Democrats working with coalitions had been wasted.

> Very often the people who are our natural allies accuse us of using them, but sometimes they use us. The environmental movement used the B.C. NDP in opposition to put forward many of its policies and positions, but now that the NDP is in government, their leadership attack us for not meeting every one of their expectations. The reality is that they've gotten a hell of a lot more than they would have with another government.
>
> The women's movement — I'm talking about NAC — very much used us when I was a member of Parliament to get access to people, to set things up for them. And we *are* feminists, in

a party with good strong feminist policies that are very much like NAC's policies. Where was NAC in the federal election? No political party met their criteria. No political party did anything or said anything that was of any value. No leader supported any position that NAC supported ... They were busy being non-partisan and saying 'no-bo-dee reflects our views'...

The labour movement better understand that when they get into these coalitions, and when the crunch comes and the reality of politics sets in, these other groups won't be there with them. They'll be non-partisan. I found it hard to go to labour-coalition things in Central Canada where the party couldn't be mentioned because everything was non-partisan. Screw it. Quite frankly, screw it.[25]

History has backed the NDP into a corner. Legislatures are less powerful than they once were; within legislatures, political parties compete for influence with lobby groups. A few New Democrats have argued that, as a party of social change, the NDP has no choice but to form close ties with the rising social action movements. However, many issue groups are partly funded by government and thus prevented from becoming partisan. Besides, almost all have declared that a formal partisan link would detract from their organizing and lobbying work.

Frustration at this dilemma has provoked a backlash in the remnant of the NDP. Long-time party members complain that their federal MPs have become captive to the lobby groups, without earning any political benefits. In any case, the argument goes, the support of coalition leaders is meaningless; these so-called leaders are just media-wise bureaucrats sitting in lobby information centres, distant from activists on the ground.

Michael Balagus, the former adviser to McLaughlin, adds that labour's shift to coalition politics threatens both labour's effectiveness and the NDP. "Bob White was fundamentally wrong," he says. "The NDP exists today because labour as a social movement recognized that it needed a parliamentary voice ... This is a real serious problem for the NDP. How do you address the fact that hard-core New Democrats are now putting their time, energy, creativity and money into coalitions?"[26]

The solution to this puzzle is far from obvious. However, I will venture a few suggestions.

First, the NDP's problems in opening up channels to issue groups have originated partly in its own state of disorganization. NDP caucuses spend endless hours debating national issues, but have never mounted a co-ordinated outreach effort. Second, as with its attempts to break into Quebec, the NDP has taken a short-term view of its investment of time in the extra-parliamentary groups, expecting an immediate payback. The NDP has been more patient in building links with organized labour over the years, despite many disappointments — as have the Liberals in working with ethnic and aboriginal groups.

Third, if New Democrats are concerned about a loss of activists to the issue groups, they might look at the world from an activist's point of view. The party's local chapters hibernate from election to election. Its conventions are rigged in the back rooms. Compared with some other organizations that are competing for talent, the NDP offers an inferior quality of experience.

Peter Bleyer, a coalition staff member, suggests that working in a low-profile, co-operative way with social action groups might reduce this problem in the NDP. He says many trade unions have become more democratic and more sensitive to their own processes since they joined the coalitions. This idealist's view of the social action movements — like Robert White's — brings to mind Mao's image from the years of the Long March, of a party swimming among the people like fish in the sea, absorbing the emergent values and hopes of the radical masses. "You've got to lower the flag," says Bleyer. "Burn the flag. You can't always be thinking about what's in it for the NDP."[27]

"The organized social movements are the NDP's best allies," says Judy Rebick. "For the party to marginalize those groups is suicidal. Those groups are gaining more power all the time, and they work independently in the interests of the NDP — unless the NDP pisses them off."[28]

What if we reverse the onus and put it back on Rebick? Who are the social movements' allies in Parliament, and what kind of support is that party entitled to? "The role of a coalition is to influence the public agenda or the government. The role of a political party is to implement," says Audrey McLaughlin. "I think you need both ... What I think the social movement community has to think about is, how many marches can you have and still refuse to work for the people who would implement what you're marching for? That's a question for them, not for us."[29]

The NDP would like to win the trust and the long-term support of both labour unions and social activists — based on the reality that New Democrats seeking office come from the same backgrounds and share many of the same values and experiences.

Unfortunately, the party is less trusted than ever before. The NDP's actions in provincial government, especially in Ontario, have outraged many social activists and disrupted the party's relations with labour. Many activists now doubt claims that the NDP is prepared to implement what they have marched for. As one result, the CLC voted at its 1994 convention to begin a two-year process of re-examining its ties with the NDP.

Canada's largest union, CUPE, has withdrawn its support from the Rae government, angry about the "atrocities" perpetrated in the social contract law.[30] The Canadian Auto Workers have cut off relations with the Ontario party except to funnel money to the federal NDP. The social contract, says CAW president Buzz Hargrove, is "the most vicious attack on the rights of workers to collective bargaining in the history of our province."[31] The Ontario Federation of Labour has followed suit, with some Federation affiliates vowing to defeat the NDP.

Hargrove was formerly Robert White's executive assistant at the CAW, and moved into White's chair when White left for the CLC. "The vast majority of labour law changes in Ontario have come from Liberal or Tory governments," Hargrove says, citing the Rand formula, severance pay and pension laws. "We can't be worse off with them than we are today. We've had less input with the NDP than with the Tories and Liberals."

The Auto Workers spent years raising NDP credibility in factory towns like Windsor and Oshawa. That credibility is gone, and with it some of the union's prestige among its members. Hargrove echoes a thought from White: that the party is trying to appeal to everybody and talking to nobody. "How do we convince workers the NDP's not just a middle-of-the road party?"[32]

However, some other private-sector unions want labour to strengthen its ties with the NDP. This camp, led by the Steelworkers and the Communications, Energy, and Paperworkers (CEP) has circulated a set of discussion papers criticizing an alleged Auto Workers-CUPE "alliance."

The discussion papers are generous to the Ontario NDP government, and suggest that much of the anti-NDP pressure in the unions is coming from the right, not the left. The central document says union leaders have to take some responsibility for not educating their members on pay equity, racism and other social issues.

> Working in coalitions is obviously vital, but to think that some messianic 'social movement' is waiting to emerge from these efforts alone is a sad delusion. Far more effort must be put into basic political education, training political activists, running labour candidates for nominations ...
>
> Whatever the villainy of the Rae, Harcourt, or Romanow governments, it is very clear that there are no other union- or worker-friendly parties waiting in the wings.[33]

Soon after the appearance of these documents, one of the co-authors, Dave Mackenzie, went from Steel to work as a strategist in Premier Rae's office. Another, André Foucault of the CEP, took over the presidency of the Ontario NDP, replacing Julie Davis, an officer of the now-departed Ontario Federation of Labour.

These disagreements threaten the unity of the CLC, although there is still a reserve of respect and mutual interest on all sides. For the NDP, the split in labour makes it very difficult to predict the outcome of the CLC's review of its relationship with the NDP, and thus the party's future. Robert White — whose performance as CLC president, by the way, has disappointed many former fans — remains cool in public to the NDP, and urged the party not to forget its socialist roots at its first post-election council meeting. If he decides to intervene in the CLC's review process, White will certainly pitch for a more socialist and more socially active party. The Steelworkers and their allies take a different line on policy and a more traditional view of party organization. Organized labour is a key source of financial support for the NDP in its period of crisis; the CLC's report will weigh heavily in future party decisions.

The mainstream media advise the party to cut its formal ties to labour. John Dafoe, of the anti-NDP *Winnipeg Free Press*, presents two arguments. First, he says, the unions have become steadily more conservative in defending their own gains, and this conservatism clashes with the NDP's message of social change. Second, he says, the NDP's ties with public service unions through the CLC bring it into a conflict-of-interest position when the party forms a government. (Dafoe does not mention the massive business donations to other parties.)[34] A 1987 Angus Reid survey suggested that the public may agree; 71 per cent of those polled opposed the idea of unions giving money to the NDP, with 20 per cent in favour. Among union members, the score was 72-20; even among self-declared NDP voters, Reid found 62 per cent against, 31 per cent in favour.[35]

New Democrats resent the corporate media posing as the conscience of the NDP, and many still believe the formal link with labour provides a net advantage. A U.K. Labour Party report on this topic offers some ideas on labour's importance to the NDP in Canada. The document mentions labour's reinforcement of values that are important to the party, such as equality. Labour brings "a practical approach based on their ground level experience," and keeps the party in touch with a "social base." Also important, for a party that gets minimal support from corporations, is labour's experience in running campaigns.[36]

Up until now, the political programs of the CLC and the NDP have been virtually identical. Both sides have faced similar tactical problems, starting with the challenge of reaching working people through the static of the mass media, and it has made sense for them to work together. Judy Darcy of CUPE says this should continue: "The focus has been far too much on the organizational relationship at the top, and not enough on the common education that needs to be done with union members and people in Canada around the programs that the NDP and the labour movement have in common ... We're not reaching our members with those issues between elections. It's no wonder we're not persuading them at election time."[37]

If the CLC unions can resolve their differences, it will produce a new period of vigour in organized labour. Through working with the coalitions, the unions are developing a more progressive, outward-looking image and leadership; in their new emphasis on private-sector productivity and public-sector reform, they are handing the NDP a more realistic set of policies to campaign on. Unfortunately, where one union welcomes an economic plan as "realistic," another may call it surrender. Robert White may think it necessary for the party, labour and social activists to build a radical base of public opinion before taking power, even if it takes decades; his critics in labour may dismiss this dream as utopian, and more importantly, empty of content.

Ideally, the New Democratic Party would play a unique and essential role among the institutions of the Canadian left, as the parliamentary arm of a broad, mature and disciplined movement for social change. By earning the trust its partners, it could build bridges among different sectors, ease the way for trade-offs and compromises among groups (labour and others) whose interests conflict, point out the damage done by capitalism run wild, help set a direction for change, and tilt any favouritism towards the poor and the disadvantaged.

In reality, the party's role is unclear. In its own renewal process, launched in the summer of 1994, it has undertaken to improve its understanding of the "special interest" communities. A party discussion paper asks whether the issue groups are "part of the problem or part of the solution."[38] The point is, I believe, that they are an increasing force in the political landscape, at a time when party organizations are retreating to the margins of power. Without waxing lyrical about their potential as a mass movement of the left, I think it is essential to recognize that the issue groups can teach the party a great deal.

The party renewal process will also examine the NDP's links with labour, although in the short term this matter rests mostly with the CLC. The Congress report due in 1996 could result in anything from foreclosure to abandonment. The party, in its weakened state, has become dependent on the CLC and its major union supporters in a way it never was before.

There are many reasons for New Democrats to hope that the party and the unions can come to an agreement that recognizes both the potential and the limitations of their relationship. The potential includes the possible role of the party as a forum for discussions on issues that affect labour, such as workplace change, pension funds, incomes policy, deficits and public service efficiency, all of which have been out of bounds in the past. The limitations include the recognition that trade unions do not represent all of the working class or the middle class, and the party has other interests to serve. NDP governments can protect the right of people to organize and strengthen the role of unions in the economy, but they cannot function as trade union governments.

In recent years, labour has increasingly claimed the freedom to differ with the NDP in public. "If we take the idea of social democracy seriously," Buzz Hargrove wrote of the Rae government, "then we have a *responsibility* to criticize this government, challenge it, make demands on it, and yes, mobilize against its direction."[39] If the left wants to avoid the shocks that inevitably follow long periods of denial, New Democrats outside labour must be free to return the favour.

9

The Virtue of Patience

The best way to foretell the future is to recall the past.
— Fortune cookie, Ottawa, April 19, 1994

The federal NDP all but disappeared from the news in the months after the 1993 election. Its financial picture worsened, and major creditors went unpaid; 310 Somerset Street West in Ottawa, purchased in 1989 to house a booming operation, now sat almost empty. The party had the choice of paying $30,000 a month to keep the three-storey building or selling it at a loss of at least $600,000.

The Council meeting of January 1994 provided a slight lift, with the appointment of a renewal committee "with a long time frame and an unlimited scope to examine all aspects of the party."[1] The committee included co-chairs Dawn Black from British Columbia and François Côté from Quebec, as well as Lorne Nystrom from Saskatchewan, Nova Scotia party leader Alexa McDonough, Winnie Ng from Toronto and youth president Maya Russell. There were also scattered signs of life outside the formal renewal process. In Alberta and Nova Scotia, provincial parties held regional meetings to discuss the federal party's future. In Toronto, some young activists and academics calling themselves the "Zoo Democrats" set up a computer forum on NDP renewal. The Ontario private-sector unions organized a conference on bringing the labour rank and file into the NDP. Some dissident trade unionists, meanwhile, planned a June convention on the founding of a new party.

The renewal committee organized six subcommittees to examine the party's mission, party structure, links with labour and social action movements, the economy, social policy and globalization. A workbook mailed out from headquarters to local NDP chapters and trade union affiliates promised that all aspects of operations and policy would come under review, an assurance that Audrey McLaughlin repeated in her speeches. On the question of the party's mission, for example, the workbook raised the following arguments:

"We have to define ourselves in a way that is sustainable in government."

"It's time we came to grips with the real world. We're not doing anyone any favours by pretending we have easy answers."

"In the transformation from the industrial to the information age we haven't re-defined the working class — i.e. the group we represent."

"People who are alienated from the system see us as another bunch of cynical politicians. We've got to change that."[2]

In mid-April, McLaughlin threw the process into temporary confusion with the announcement of her intention to resign at some unstated point in the future. Up to this point, the leader had declined to comment on her long-term plans. It was clear, though, that an immediate departure followed by an early leadership convention would cause problems. Several prospective leadership candidates had no seat in Parliament, and almost no chance of getting one for at least three years. As well, a full-blown leadership race at the scheduled August convention would overshadow the renewal process.

However, the party constitution was clear on the rules governing leadership votes. The constitution required that the executive call a convention every two years, and this one was already a year overdue. At a convention, any New Democrat was free to contest the leadership. Some speculated that McLaughlin would name an interim leader, probably Nelson Riis, and ask the convention to confirm him as a caretaker until just before the next federal election.

On April 18, 1994, McLaughlin met with the table officers of the federal NDP in an Ottawa hotel. After three hours behind closed doors, she emerged into a room packed with reporters and announced that she had submitted her notice of resignation. Nobody had pressured her to go, she said; many people had asked her to stay. She would lead the party through the renewal period, but not into another election. She wanted to be perfectly clear. She wanted an honest, open process.

In their remarks to the media, McLaughlin and party president Nancy Riche left out a few details. They failed to mention, for instance, that they had just suspended the party constitution, cancelled the summer convention, and extended their own terms in office indefinitely. Party members only learned of these things when convention staff — executing their last task prior to layoff — phoned local NDP presidents to pass on the news.

By the official account, the table officers had cancelled the convention because the Federal Council wanted a new method for electing the next leader, and it would take time to work out the details. Informally, executive members said they had made their move in order to save money and avoid the televised embarrassment of a potentially half-empty hall. They had acted to help the party. What kind of party? One where the leader and executive could rule by decree, and extend their own terms at will?

Delia Carley, a quiet-spoken social activist and a former MP's assistant, spoke out for indignant party members. She wrote in *The Ottawa Citizen* that the executive group had put the party into "moral receivership ... Would union members sit still if, following a disastrous strike, a labour leader cancelled union elections?"[3]

The decisions of April 18 also cost the renewal committee its high-profile convention launch and its staff co-ordinator. Co-chairs Black and Côté travelled to Ottawa to meet with McLaughlin. They discussed plans for a summer policy conference that would serve as a pseudo-substitute for the lost convention. Some former caucus researchers volunteered to pull together subcommittee meetings and prepare discussion papers. Through the rest of the spring, members of the renewal team continued to predict that they would conduct a wide-ranging, no-holds-barred review of party affairs.

McLaughlin, after her hour before the cameras, returned to the obscurity of her small Parliament Hill office and her nine-member caucus, each caucus member as stubbornly independent as ever. Her calendar of engagements was now almost blank. At a June meeting of the full NDP executive, McLaughlin again offered to resign, and her offer was declined once more. The executive scheduled the next party convention for October 1995. It also decided, reluctantly, to end the temporary funding that had allowed McLaughlin to keep extra staff on the Hill beyond what Parliament would provide for an ordinary MP. As of July 1, she would lose two of her four Ottawa assistants.

So the federal New Democratic Party sets out to renew itself. It has the advantage of a large membership in British Columbia, Saskatchewan, Manitoba and Ontario. Its widespread popularity as recently as 1991 suggests there is still a potential social democratic base across the country, even if current levels of public support are extremely low. Think of the NDP as a familiar landmark — an established hotel, recently fallen on hard times, plenty of empty rooms. Maybe the owners — in this case, some provincial parties and some trade unions — neglected it. Maybe a succession of managers misjudged their market, maybe the neighbourhood around it has changed. Who will save this landmark from the wrecker's ball?

The responsibility for rescuing the NDP, or letting it die, is in fact widely dispersed. It can only survive as the electoral expression, fully realized and articulated, of a broader movement. The party has weathered a long siege in capitalist North America. It was bolstered in the community and the workplace by idealists who stepped forward, generation after generation, to speak for an alternative system of values. In recent years, the NDP has ceased to matter to many of these people — partly because of a certain cold opportunism in its governments and its election operations, partly because of divisions in organized labour, partly because the growing social action movements insist on appearing non-partisan, sending the message that the NDP is the same as other parties. Nobody can predict whether Canadian workers and dreamers will again find common cause, overcome their distaste for politics, and build an informed electoral majority for social change in this splintered country. New Democrats can consult with the experts and survey public opinion before they renovate the old hotel; they cannot predict how many customers will show up.

Audrey McLaughlin and her supporters recognized the need for party renewal during the leadership contest of 1989. For all my impatience with McLaughlin, I believe many of her early proposals deserve a second chance. Many of these dealt with how people *experience* the party, whether they find it to be honest, open, democratic, respectful to them. McLaughlin founded her regime on the idea that Canadians wanted a new politics and that the NDP could take advantage of this public demand. She led the NDP to a crushing defeat at the hands of two masters of traditional politics, Jean Chrétien and Preston Manning. Her instinct was sound, but she lacked the ability, and perhaps the support in the party, to convince the public she had something new to say. Her style of leadership was perceived as the absence of leadership, the abdication of personal authority.

McLaughlin expected to find the most receptive audience for the new politics among the 100,000 or more dues-paying New Democrats across Canada. She suggested that the membership should get first priority as a constituency to be consulted and informed. However, the federal party's success in putting McLaughlin's words into action was marginal. The party and caucus continued to communicate through anonymously addressed mailings to millions of households. As far as the members could tell, the new politics was mostly a figment of McLaughlin's imagination.

The NDP functions, to varying extents, as a debating club, a social action organization, a centre for the adaptation of ideas to Canadian government, an electoral machine, a party in Parliament. In each of these areas it has always claimed to act as a democratic organization, sensitive to the wishes of its membership. The NDP must determine what this claim means in the 1990s: money, time, the accountability of officers, patience, education, the development of new skills. "There is almost an infinite appetite for more democracy, more involvement by citizens. Democracy is not just about preparing for elections; it is about making more democracy every day of our lives," says former Yukon NDP leader Tony Pennikett.[4] "What the political system suffers from is lack of debate," says former Toronto mayor John Sewell. "The left in Canada has always begun that debate. It doesn't mean we always get it right, but we put things on the table and get people talking about the issues."[5]

The federal NDP does not have infinite resources to spend on its members, but it could certainly make better use of the resources it has. The party has survived from election to election as a body of campaign volunteers and temporary organizers knit together by a few paid strategists and MPs. It has never hired a qualified professional manager with a background in running a large institution. It has never hired a professional fundraiser or had a fundraising plan. Its finance committee is made up of the treasurers of provincial parties, which often compete directly with the federal party for funds. Its expensive one-of-a-kind computer database is too complicated for staff to understand; for many months, headquarters had to call in the designer (at a high hourly rate) every time it wanted to send mail to a new list of people. In summary, the federal party skimps on corporate development between elections and then goes wild during campaigns using borrowed money ($3 million in 1993).

In a more prudently run organization, there might be more resources available for work with the membership. I will not overstate the enthusiasm of the average member; most simply want to be left alone. However, there is a wide scope for work by active members between elections, beyond serving on party councils.

It is conceivable, in an abstract way, that a party could survive without members. Paid staff already play a dominant role in raising money, writing policy and planning elections. The armies of election-time volunteers are becoming irrelevant; Joy Langan had by far the biggest campaign in Mission-Coquitlam, but she came third, an experience shared by candidates across Canada. "Election day we were the only ones pulling the vote, and we were pulling people who didn't vote for us."[6] However, a party that believes in the practical value of democracy should be looking for new opportunities to make use of a loyal and informed following. With the kind of volunteer training done by other organizations, the NDP's active members could raise the party's profile by representing the New Democrat position within unions and community groups, or even by debating with each other in public. Even a few hundred committed activists working in this way would represent a potent force. Political economist Duncan Cameron says the NDP has largely neglected this opportunity.

> In the past decade, the left has lost the battle for public opinion. We don't own or control the media, and we don't take ideas and research and stuff seriously. Most Canadians don't know the basic distribution of wealth in this country. They don't know there are 3 million unemployed. Unless you get some basic framing of issues and questions going on all the time, you'll never get to public opinion ...
>
> It would be great to have public meetings where New Democrats were asking Reformers how they're going to save democracy when wealth and decision-making power are all controlled by eight families and two conglomerates and six chartered banks. Let's talk about that part of democracy.[7]

Many critics have urged the party to do more extra-parliamentary work; in this book, I have said that the federal NDP caucus could have worked more effectively with other groups on selected campaigns, for example against NAFTA. The party councils will always insist, rightly, that this work should fit with the party's chief task, which is to elect people to Parliament. The NDP can be faulted for exaggerating the importance of Parliament and downgrading the work of groups active in other areas. Even so, Parliament retains symbolic and real powers, starting with the power to spend tax money.

At present, the NDP is reduced to non-party status in the Commons. Its MPs ask two short questions a week at most, have no status on committees and get little exposure in the media. Can it win back a third of the voters in its former areas of strength and recover some seats? Perhaps it can. Moving beyond its long-term plateau of 30-odd seats would be a different matter.

In one view, the correct strategic response to 1993 is clear. The federal NDP can only recover if it again adopts the pragmatic approach of successful parties in British Columbia, Saskatchewan and possibly Manitoba. Each of these provinces has its own political history — in Saskatchewan and British Columbia, the Liberals have been very weak in the past — but in all cases, the NDP crowds the centre, knowing that the other parties will not normally outflank the New Democrats on the left. This, in the conventional view, was the Broadbent strategy — to cultivate a moderate and reassuring image, and to spread the word that "the Liberals are Tories too," perhaps implying that the New Democrats were the true Liberals.

This strategy for attracting voters may have boosted Broadbent's popularity in 1987, although it did not carry him to power against John Turner. The team that advised McLaughlin, including Les Campbell and pollster David Gotthilf, proposed a different strategy. In their view, the federal NDP should look for its support from left-of-centre voters and present itself as an innovative, creative and radical contrast to the Liberals. The NDP would be the we-try-harder party, tight, disciplined, leading the way on the tough issues. Like several other concepts from the McLaughlin era, this approach was not broadly or clearly articulated. And, like several other concepts, it had trouble finding a footing in reality. The federal NDP did not fit the strategy, since it was not innovative or creative. The party showed flashes of intensity and a fair degree of unity in its parliamentary work, but it never reached an overall strategic consensus.

The Campbell-Gotthilf approach had some attractive features. It counselled the NDP to anticipate major developments as well as responding to events and the decisions of other parties. It raised the crucial question of the NDP's long-term future: how can a political party make itself disciplined, responsive, poised to take power, and yet be democratic and engage in consultation?

Under the current party structure, however, the federal NDP is very unlikely to take an independent radical direction. Powerful provincial leaders will tolerate populist Us-and-Them rhetoric, but they do not want to answer for the doings of an alien body. As shareholders in the federal party they have influence over funding, party staff, MPs and federal councillors, and they will use that influence to keep the federal party in check. Under the present balance of power in the party, the next federal leader may well be restricted to something like the Broadbent strategy.

Meanwhile, the NDP's near-disappearance is good news for the Liberal Party. They have a chance to consolidate their new presence in the West, where their historic weakness helped make room for the NDP to flourish in the past. The Liberals already have significant strength among aboriginal and multicultural leaders; the architect of their 1993 campaign Red Book is a former president of NAC. It is possible that, within a decade, labour and social activists will have adopted the Liberal Party as their permanent home, as their counterparts live under the Democrat umbrella in the United States. With this possibility in mind, many New Democrats were perversely pleased with the Chrétien government's shuffle to the right in its first year, its speedy endorsement of NAFTA and its scaling back of job creation.

The NDP's woes are also a sign of hope for anyone who has prayed for the appearance of a new party. Various would-be charismatic figures will be weighing their odds of becoming the Preston Manning of the left. Nationalists, greens, socialists all know that political conditions are shifting from week to week, and voters try new parties as they might try a new cereal or a colour of paint. In the view of political scientist James Laxer, this volatility will heat up as we enter the late 1990s. He predicts a cultural sea-change related to computer networks and the control of information, virtual reality, feminism and the global ecosystem. The one-time 60s radical looks forward with relish to this period.

> I think the X generation is going to do it because they *have* to do it. The big players are going to be people we've never heard of, and their formulations are going to be formulations we've never heard of ...
>
> My sense is that it's going to be a worldwide phenomenon. It's going to be as culturally bizarre for the baby boomers as

what happened in the 1960s was to their parents, but it's going to happen ...

Young people are going to figure out that painfully doing what society tells them to do, and running faster and harder, will not get them what they've been promised. Gradually, in ways that nobody can predict, they'll figure it out. The first response will be a cultural response. Then all of a sudden NAFTA and the multinational corporations will be on the defensive.[8]

In the world where every local group is part of a global computer linkup, there will be international demands on a party of the left, diverse regional demands, and a need for a wide range of state-of-the-art marketing methods. And there will still be a requirement, in the face of global economic pressures, for a national economic plan to generate high-skill jobs. This scenario suggests strong advantages for an innovative and creative national party; it is less favourable for a party run as a joint venture by three or four provincial sections.

John Sewell, who works as a political consultant and agitator in Toronto, says that parties on the left will have to learn to fine-tune their responses to provide different "correct" answers for different situations and groups. They will share with the social action movements a trust in the value of small transformations in communities, work environments and individual lives. "What seemed to be the answers 20 years ago don't work. That is, the big answers don't work. I think there's a whole lot of small answers ... This is one of the lessons governments haven't learned that companies have."[9]

Peter Julian, a young British Columbian who works at the NDP outpost in Montreal, suggests parties in the next era will be measured by their success in providing a political home, by their way of doing things, their commitment to working with people on their terms. "If we build it, they will come," says Julian about people now entering the work force. "There's terrible frustration there. And unless there's a political focus, I think there will just be continuing frustration — or they'll go for groups that rely on symbols with no substance ... But if we don't know where we're going, how do we expect people to follow us?"[10]

There will be NDP names on some ballots in the next federal election. The NDP still has more than 180 elected members in provincial legislatures and hundreds more political staff. If the Rae and Har-

court governments are defeated, this partisan energy will disperse,
but some will collect at the federal level. Regardless of what happens
at Somerset Street, five or six provincial sections will fight regional
campaigns.

These campaigns will offer a common agenda that is both familiar
and distinctive. Audrey McLaughlin summed it up in a speech to the
1994 Canadian Labour Congress convention.

> Together we are part of a movement based on a vision. A vision
> of freedom, freedom for ourselves and others. The words of J.S.
> Woodsworth remain as true today as decades ago — that what
> we desire for ourselves, we wish also for others. What does this
> vision mean in practice?
>
> • A commitment to trade unionism;
> • To equality between men and women;
> • An end to racial discrimination;
> • Freedom from violence, from war;
> • Freedom from want with a commitment to eliminate poverty
>   and to work for full employment;
> • A commitment to future generations through a sustainable
>   environment.[11]

This list of good intentions displays a continuity with the past and
an awareness of current issues. It speaks to labour, to feminists,
people from visible minorities, social activists, environmentalists. It
is not strictly a "vision of freedom," though; it owes more to the
concept of solidarity. As an Israeli party document puts it, "A life of
freedom and equality is possible only when one person supports the
other and desires the other's freedom."[12] McLaughlin's list, so easily
accepted at first glance, calls on people to give and take. This is
where the real problems begin.

McLaughlin said in an interview that the NDP still has a vision;
but she worries that New Democrats are troubled, demoralized,
doubting that their vision "works in the real world."[13] I would say
that rather than being demoralized, the left is badly divided. There
may be 30 or 40 per cent of the population, New Democrats, former
New Democrats and others, who accept the above list, but this still
leaves room for deep disagreement on fundamental issues.

I will mention two areas of division among many, leaving out the
question of Quebec. First, the above agenda skips over the question

of the party's attitude to the private sector. Second, it does not address the wide-ranging conflicts dividing people with a feminist or other equality-seeking orientation from more traditional or populist NDP voters.

On the first point, I have referred earlier to the confusion within the NDP about socialist versus social democratic perspectives on the economy. It is unfair and unwise to ask voters to support the party until some of this confusion is resolved. Recent campaign themes, in an attempt to win votes from everywhere, leave room for the idea that the NDP is or should be a socialist party, bent on the liquidation of capitalism. This idea has wide currency among federal New Democrats and ex-New Democrats. McLaughlin's list offers no guidance one way or the other.

Leading figures on the left, such as coalition activist Tony Clarke, would like to see the NDP stiffen its corporate-bashing rhetoric.

> The corporate welfare bums theme has to be taken off the shelf, dusted off, and brought back with a huge force, so that people can see who's calling the shots. For the last 10 years, we have formally had in place a corporate agenda, and it's still there ...
>
> A party that wants to be in government has to work out its program for handling the corporations long before it is elected. The gross and harmful effects of the market are going to show themselves for what they are, and there's going be a swing back towards re-regulation. What will a new and revitalized public sector look like?[14]

Others, including myself, will argue that the while the NDP must support the effective regulation and taxation of big business, as well as new forms of ownership, the party must also be clear on the role of the private sector. In a mixed economy, no government will pretend it can eliminate profits, competition or individual economic ambition. As Ed Broadbent put it in a 1991 essay, " 'moral incentives' as the driving force in an economy have never been sufficient to produce beyond the subsistence level. Why believe they ever will?"[15]

The weight of academic, government and political thinking around the NDP lies with the social democratic course, with a program designed to extract maximum public benefits from a mixed economy built on a productive private sector, minimum unemployment, increased accountability by corporate managers to workers and communities, balanced government budgets, and an accountable, responsive, efficient public sector delivering programs to the people who need them. This program will not, by itself, deliver the excitement needed to beat the Liberals. It is, however, compatible with McLaughlin's six points, and it answers some urgent questions about what the NDP wants to *do*. It also sends a message that the NDP has the ability to go beyond analysis and offer solutions.

Can the socialist left in the NDP work with a social democratic program? If not, will the NDP split or continue to fudge its economic position? Doug Coupar, the co-chair of a party renewal subcommittee, express a fear that New Democrats in the post-1993 period are more tempted than ever to talk only about medicare and other social policy issues, and "abdicate the responsibility for putting together an economic program."[16]

McLaughlin's six-point list has another, perhaps even more serious failing. The phrase that supposedly binds the list, "what we desire for ourselves, we wish for others," comes apart over moral and cultural differences. What one family wants may be totally inappropriate for its neighbours. The question of what kind of people a left party should serve — either a feminist, internationalist, pro-equality base, or culturally more conservative populists — remains unresolved.

"What has brought freshness and inspiration to our party in the past couple of decades," says former Yukon NDP leader Tony Pennikett, "are the ideas of the women's movement and the environmental movement."[17] These ideas have found a place in the NDP, agrees James Laxer; unfortunately, many party members now "look down their noses at the guys on the assembly line reading page 3 of the *Sun*," who along with farmers, miners and loggers were "the foundation of Canadian social democracy,"[18] McLaughlin's final-ballot showdown against Dave Barrett in 1989 reflected this division, although imperfectly, and the fault line ran through McLaughlin's 44-member federal caucus.

This elusive division — flaring up for a moment in conversation and then fading away — shows itself in differences between women and men, downtown and rural/suburban dwellers, middle-class social activists pushing for change and working families fighting to keep what they have. Most New Democrats have loyalties on both sides of the line — for example, Joy Langan, the veteran trade unionist and feminist, or Howard McCurdy, the scientist and human rights advocate who represented an auto workers' riding. But there is

enough ill feeling and insecurity at each extreme to threaten the
future of an uncertain party. Elsewhere on the left, labour leaders and
social activists are working to bridge the same gap in their coalitions.
The jury is still out on whether they can succeed.

Working families, Ed Broadbent's "ordinary Canadians," are on
the run, and the NDP, in focusing all its resources on election planning, has lost touch with them. For half a generation, governments
have wilfully created unemployment and wrecked communities. The
percentage of Canada's private-sector work force covered by union
contracts fell from 31 per cent in 1968 to 18 per cent in 1990, and is
still falling.[19] Men who once felt secure in good jobs now hunt for
low-paying positions. They can no longer support their families,
they're angry about it, and often blame the women and immigrants
they jostle with in the labour market. Many Canadian workers have
lived, says MP Chris Axworthy, in a grey area between bigotry and
tolerance; under present conditions, they are at best indifferent to the
problems of aboriginals, the disabled or people on welfare. They are
hoping for practical improvements in their own lives.

> People had said to the NDP, okay, you can speak for gay and
> lesbian rights if you want, as long as you're holding on to our
> health care system and fighting the banks. But once they
> thought we weren't saying anything on the economy, they
> turfed us on the other things. Plus, the Reform Party made
> them feel good about their bigotry. We made them feel bad.[20]

In much of the West, frustrated former NDP voters turned in large
numbers in 1993 to the Reform Party; party opinion surveys suggest
that women aged 45 to 64 led the way. Preston Manning's party
offered simple economic prescriptions and some Us-and-Them theatre pitting ordinary folks against government. It worked. Some New
Democrats want to copy the newer party, with its swagger, its formulas and its roots in popular emotion. Nelson Riis, the only surviving NDP MP from the B.C. interior, played to this feeling in April
1994 when he speculated on the chances for a parliamentary alliance
between the two parties.

Reform's economic cure would be worse than the disease, and its
promise of internal democracy is false. Even so, Reform claims with
some credibility to have replaced the NDP as the cultural and moral
voice of working families and their communities. Gerry Scott, a
former B.C. NDP secretary and a long-time activist in the federal

party, blames a double élitism in the NDP — the élitism of political big shots and the behaviour of a self-appointed moral élite who follow political fashion.

> The evidence of these trends are quite clear ... the convention debates controlled by paid staff with walkie-talkies; the refusal of our caucus to seriously question the perks, pensions and overseas junkets that sicken the public, including a large number of people who used to work for us; the willingness to characterize every potential Reform supporter as a rich Albertan with "redneck" views ... A more serious factor in our isolation from our mass base is the refusal of the federal party to address controversial issues that we simply do not like to address. In this category I would like to place 'law and order'/community safety, immigration, social responsibility and social values (as opposed to individual rights), bilingualism ... In all of these instances, and too many more, the federal NDP has demonstrated one consistent approach: We Know Best. To Hell With the Public.[21]

These are valid concerns, but very angry statements. They demand a high price for freedom of debate. Scott wants the NDP to endure "a period of anarchy where people talk about what they believe" in the media and elsewhere.[22] Those who chose to take part could speak stridently and in wounding terms: racist, politically correct, reactionary, special rights. All sides would claim the support of most voters, as well as the moral high ground.

The evidence suggests that the various interests that maintained the federal NDP have set out in different directions. The party can only attempt, in an approximate or brokering way, to find compromises. This will require debate and negotiation among party and trade union and community leaders, as well as intelligence and goodwill.

Unfortunately, the NDP's identity as a party of the downtrodden has bred a unique brand of self-indulgence that threatens the chances for unity. There are, obviously, many downtrodden Canadians. However, building a party and labelling it "for the downtrodden" produces strange outcomes. People argue over who is more aggrieved. The party decides, understandably, that all expressions of suffering should be treated equally. Organizations then compete with money and influence to make sure they produce the most and the loudest expressions of suffering. The richest win.

At a certain point, claims of victimization become abuse of power. An NDP that is overloaded with self-appointed victims will blow itself up. In reality, many who have the means to work within a political party are privileged people. They are wasting the party's energy if they enter the debate only to settle personal scores. The feminist professors, the trade union reps, the members of party councils have won considerable freedom to make choices in their own lives, and they bear the responsibility of leadership. This includes putting into practice the key values of the party, most especially the value of solidarity, often expressed in the phrase "an injury to one is an injury to all." Self-interest and the general interest are intertwined. A power structure that promotes discrimination, poverty, violence or environmental ruin will recoil on everyone. There is no time to quarrel over who is angriest.

Let me conclude with two admonitions from Audrey McLaughlin. The first is to acknowledge the power we have and to use it carefully as a gift. The second is to listen, and skip the accusations.

> I hope that in the debates that we have, at the kitchen table or elsewhere, that we will begin to discipline ourselves. Because we're very bad. We're very judgemental. How do we jump from A to B on some of this? "You said you're concerned about loggers. Guess you don't care about the environment." We're very bad for that.[23]

The New Democratic Party no longer offers visions of a New Jerusalem. At its best — more often than these pages would suggest — the party is place where like-minded people can work together for social change. I hope, as the global cultural turbulence increases, that New Democrats will further cultivate the virtue of patience. The person standing in front of us is usually not the cause of our problems. The radical preacher Salem Bland once advised an audience of social democrats to go easy on each other and remember the common purpose. "We must be patient in explaining," he said, "but indomitable in criticism."[24]

I also hope the NDP can supplement its good intentions with some investment in ideas and innovation, and some genuine interchange with non-party organizations. I apologize, at the end, for not having identified "It" — the exciting issue or promise that will rocket the NDP back to popularity. I can suggest, however, that "It" will be useless if it is regarded just as a tool for central committees. "It" must be passed on in an intensive, detailed way to an active core of members and refined for use in different regions and communities on the left. "It" will be tied up somehow with a decision to work in an ongoing way for more democracy in the party and the parliamentary system.

New Democrats, union and social activists, are an impatient lot. There is much to dislike in the NDP, as with any institution rooted in the muck of politics and government. But turning one's back on government will not make it go away, and marches on the lawn in front of Parliament are not enough. A seat in the Commons is a prize worth having; a social democratic government in Ottawa would be better still. Neither OXFAM nor the Playwrights Union appears ready to run candidates. The job is left to the NDP.

Notes

Introduction
1. Insight Canada survey, analysed in Jon Pammett, "Tracking the Votes," in Alan Frizzell, Jon Pammett, and Anthony Westell, eds., *The Canadian Election 1993* (Ottawa: Carleton University Press, 1994).
2. Fraser Green, report to NDP Federal Council, January 29, 1984.
3. Audrey McLaughlin, mailing to NDP convention delegates, July 14, 1989.
4. The Insight survey shows that, given a long list of issues, 49 per cent of those surveyed chose "jobs" as the most important issue in 1993. Of these, 61 per cent reported voting Liberal as opposed to 4 per cent NDP.
5. Remarks to a conference of private-sector unions, Toronto, May 6, 1994.

Chapter 1
1. "The New Ideal and the New Party," notes at the United Church Archives, Toronto, reconstructed by Ian McLeod.
2. Examples: Federal leader Tommy Douglas lost in Regina in the party's first election in 1962; in fact, Saskatchewan produced no seats for the NDP in three straight elections. The party lost 9 of 11 federal seats in British Columbia in 1968, and Douglas went down to personal defeat again. Leader David Lewis lost his Toronto seat in 1974 along with almost half his caucus. The 1988 result, where the NDP got more seats than ever before, was experienced as a huge defeat because of high expectations.
3. *The Ottawa Citizen,* editorial, October 31, 1993.
4. James S. Woodsworth, "Towards Socialism," 1916, Glenbow Archives, Calgary (pamphlet).
5. "Regina Manifesto," Appendix to Kenneth McNaught, *A Prophet in Politics* (Toronto: University of Toronto Press, 1959).
6. Ed Broadbent, retirement speech, 1989, in Leo Heaps, ed., *Our Canada: The Story of the New Democratic Party Yesterday, Today and Tomorrow* (Toronto: Lorimer, 1991), p. 196.
7. James Laxer interview, January 25, 1994.
8. James Laxer, *Rethinking the Economy* (Toronto: NC Press, 1984), p. 80.
9. Guy Standing, "Fragmented Flexibility," in Daniel Drache, ed., *Getting on Track: Social Democratic Strategies for Ontario* (Kingston: McGill-Queen's University Press, 1992).
10. Ed Broadbent, "Social Democracy and Canada's Future," in Heaps, ed., *Our Canada,* p. 191.
11. Nelson Riis interview, January 26, 1994.
12. Tony Clarke interview, January 31, 1994.
13. Gerry Scott interview, February 15, 1994.
14. Peter Bleyer interview, January 28, 1994.
15. Howard McCurdy, remarks to NDP Federal Council, January 29, 1994.
16. Daniel Drache interview, January 25, 1994.
17. Desmond Morton, letter to Ian McLeod, November 23, 1993.
18. Doug Coupar interview, January 11, 1994.
19. Lynn McDonald, *The Party That Changed Canada* (Toronto: Macmillan of Canada, 1987), p. 224.

20. Joseph Wearing, *Strained Relations* (Toronto: McClelland & Stewart, 1988), p. 174.
21. John Richards and Don Kerr, eds., *Canada: What's Left?* (Edmonton: NeWest Press, 1986), p. 10.
22. George Ehring and Wayne Roberts, *Giving Away a Miracle* (Oakville: Mosaic Press, 1993), pp. 11, 176–182.
23. See Jill Vickers, Pauline Rankin, and Christine Appelle, *Politics As If Women Mattered: A Political Analysis of the National Action Committee on the Status of Women* (Toronto: University of Toronto Press, 1993), Chapters 5 and 6.
24. Bill Knight interview, March 2, 1994.
25. Alan Whitehorn, *Canadian Socialism: Essays on the CCF-NDP* (Toronto: Oxford University Press,1992), p. 29.
26. Marion Dewar interview, January 14, 1994.
27. Nelson Riis interview, January 26, 1994.

Chapter 2

1. "Political Parties and Ideologies in Canada," in Alain G. Gagnon and A. Brian Tanguay, eds., *Canadian Parties in Transition* (Scarborough: Nelson Canada, 1991), p. 60.
2. Alan Gregg, quoted in Wearing, *Strained Relations,* p. 107.
3. Jill Vickers interview, March 8, 1994.
4. It was actually Douglas's NDP successor in Saskatchewan, Woodrow Lloyd, who put medicare into effect.
5. Stephen Lewis interview, September 9, 1985.
6. T.C. Douglas interview, May 14, 1985.
7. See Whitehorn, *Canadian Socialism,* pp. 191–192.
8. Lorne Nystrom interview, February 2, 1994.
9. Desmond Morton, *The New Democrats 1961–1986* (Toronto: Copp Clark Pitman, 1986), p. 217.
10. Gerald Caplan memo, quoted in Graham Fraser, *Playing for Keeps* (Toronto: McClelland & Stewart, 1989) p. 118.
11. Fraser, *Playing for Keeps,* p. 118.
12. Stephen Brooks, *Canadian Democracy: An Introduction* (Toronto: McClelland & Stewart, 1993), p. 205.
13. Peter Julian interview, February 4, 1994.
14. Robert White, "Lost Opportunity: New Democrats Let Labour Down," *Our Times,* January 1989.
15. Whitehorn, *Canadian Socialism,* p. 222.
16. Ed Broadbent interview, October 25, 1985.
17. For example, see Neil Bradford, "Ideas, Intellectuals, and Social Democracy in Canada," in Gagnon and Taguay, eds., *Canadian Parties in Transition,* pp. 98–103; or Richards and Kerr, eds., *Canada: What's Left?* (Edmonton: NeWest Press, 1986).
18. James Laxer interview, January 25, 1994.
19. Pierre Graveline, "A Missed Rendez-Vous," *Our Times,* May 1989, pp. 16–17.
20. Geoffrey Stevens, Vancouver *Sun,* October 17, 1989.
21. Les MacPherson, Saskatoon *Star-Phoenix,* September 8, 1989.
22. "Speculation over NDP leadership," *The Financial Post,* February 7, 1989.
23. *The Edmonton Journal,* editorial, May 18, 1989.
24. Nelson Riis interview, January 22, 1994.
25. Audrey McLaughlin, Notes for announcement of candidacy, May 24, 1989.
26. Richard Hoffman, AM-NDP-White, Canadian Press wire service, June 4, 1989.
27. *The Toronto Star,* October 7, 1989.

28. "Lack of policy agenda dogs McLaughlin," *The Toronto Star,* November 25, 1989.
29. David Pepper interview, December 22, 1993.
30. Audrey McLaughlin, "Building a Democratic Socialist Economy," speech at Osgoode Hall, Toronto, November 21, 1989.
31. Audrey McLaughlin, nomination speech, December 1, 1989, private video.
32. Audrey McLaughlin, nomination speech.
33. Audrey McLaughlin campaign mailing to delegates, July 14, 1989.
34. Joy Langan interview, February 9, 1994.
35. Nelson Riis interview, January 26, 1994.

Chapter 3
1. Audrey McLaughlin, *A Woman's Place: My Life and Politics* (Toronto: MacFarlane Walter & Ross, 1992), p. 196.
2. Sally Armstrong, "Audrey McLaughlin," *Homemaker's Magazine,* January–February 1990.
3. Dawn Black interview, February 11, 1994.
4. Audrey McLaughlin interview, March 17, 1994.
5. Marion Dewar interview, January 14, 1994.
6. See Vickers, et al., *Politics As If Women Mattered.*
7. See Micheline de Sève, "Women, Political Action and Identity," in Colin Leys and Marguerite Mendell, *Culture and Social Change* (Montreal: Black Rose, 1992).
8. Judy Rebick interview, *Action Canada Dossier,* #37, pp. 20–21.
9. McLaughlin, *A Woman's Place,* p. 198.
10. Brooks, *Canadian Democracy* (Toronto: McClelland & Stewart, 1993), p. 346.
11. Marion Dewar interview, January 14, 1994.
12. Michael Balagus interview, January 11, 1994.
13. Jill Vickers interview, March 8, 1994.
14. Caroline Andrew conversation, April 19, 1994.
15. Dick Proctor interview, February 8, 1994.
16. Marion Dewar interview, January 14, 1994.
17. Jill Vickers interview, March 8, 1994.
18. John Lownsborough, "Sister Audrey," *Saturday Night,* May 1992.
19. Judy Rebick interview, April 8, 1994.
20. McLaughlin, *A Woman's Place,* p. 4.
21. McLaughlin, *A Woman's Place,* p. xi.
22. Michael Balagus interview, January 20, 1994.
23. Michael Balagus interview, January 20, 1994.
24. Marion Dewar interview, January 14, 1994.
25. Judy Rebick interview, April 8, 1994.
26. This is calculated to include allegedly "supplementary" questions, which are in fact distinct, stand-alone questions.
27. Michael Balagus interview, February 17, 1994.
28. Michael Balagus interview, February 17, 1994.
29. Gertrude Robinson and Armande Saint-Jean, "Women Politicians and Their Media Coverage: A Generational Analysis," in Kathy Megyery, ed., *Women in Canadian Politics,* Volume 6 of the Research Studies, Royal Commission on Electoral Reform (Toronto: Dundurn Press, 1991). See pp. 147–153.
30. Jane Taber interview, February 2, 1994.
31. Denise Harrington interview, April 12, 1994.
32. Geoffrey York interview, February 20, 1994.
33. John Walsh interview, March 28, 1994.

34. McLaughlin worked to stop air shipments of plutonium fuel over the Yukon and to prevent a ban on Canadian furs in Europe. McLaughlin, *A Woman's Place,* pp. 35–39.
35. Dick Proctor interview, February 8, 1994.
36. Dawn Black interview, Februray 10, 1994.
37. Marion Dewar interview, January 14, 1994.
38. Alan Whitehorn, notes on this manuscript, May 1994.

Chapter 4
1. Michel Agnaieff interview, February 4, 1994.
2. Phil Edmonston interview, February 22, 1994.
3. Les Campbell interview, April 5, 1994.
4. *House of Commons Debates,* February 24, 1992, p. 7494.
5. John Brewin interview, February 2, 1994.
6. For example, see Thomas H. McLeod and Ian McLeod, *Tommy Douglas: The Road to Jerusalem* (Edmonton: Hurtig, 1987), pp. 232–233.
7. Arnold Peters interview, May 29, 1985.
8. Chris Axworthy interview, March 1, 1994.
9. Audrey McLaughlin interview, March 17, 1994.
10. Dawn Black interview, February 10, 1994.
11. Joy Langan interview, February 9, 1994.
12. Michael Balagus interview, January 13, 1994.
13. Les Campbell interview, April 5, 1994.
14. David Perry interview, February 15, 1994.
15. *The Toronto Star,* "High anxiety in the NDP," June 6, 1992.
16. *The Toronto Star,* July 17, 1992.
17. Chris Axworthy interview, March 1, 1994.
18. Marion Dewar interview, January 14, 1994.
19. John Brewin interview, January 28, 1994.
20. Sandra Mitchell interview, February 7, 1994.
21. Les Campbell, memo to Audrey McLaughlin, December 14, 1992.
22. John Brewin interview, January 28, 1994. Chief critic Svend Robinson was in Baghdad for much of this period.
23. *House of Commons Debates,* January 15, 1991, p. 16999.
24. Nelson Riis interview, January 26, 1994.
25. Guy Freedman interview, March 16, 1994.
26. Brian Gardiner interview, February 10, 1994.
27. John Brewin interview, January 28, 1994.
28. Sandra Mitchell interview, February 8, 1994.
29. Sandra Mitchell interview, February 7, 1994.
30. Canadian Press report from Jill Rutherford, Whitehorse, September 21, 1989.
31. *The Toronto Star,* June 6, 1992.
32. *The Financial Post,* May 1, 1993.
33. *The Windsor Star,* April 30, 1993.
34. *The Globe and Mail,* May 7, 1993.
35. Alain Dubuc, editorial, *La Presse,* May 4, 1993.
36. Phil Edmonston interview, February 22, 1994.

Chapter 5
1. *Le Devoir,* editorial, December 7, 1989.
2. Michel Agnaieff interview, February 4, 1994.
3. *Le Devoir,* editorial, March 16, 1987.
4. Raymond Guardia interview, February 2, 1994.
5. George Nakitsas interview, March 4, 1994.

6. Michel Agnaieff interview, February 4, 1994.
7. Henry Milner, "What Canadian Social Democrats Need to Know About Sweden, and Why," in John Richards, Robert Cairns, and Larry Pratt, eds., *Social Democracy Without Illusions* (Toronto: McClelland & Stewart, 1991), p. 76.
8. See Daniel Drache and Meric Gertler, "The World Economy and the Nation-State," in Drache and Gertler, eds., *The New Era of Global Competition* (Kingston: McGill-Queen's University Press, 1991), pp. 15–17.
9. The current deputy federal secretary, Raymond Guardia, suggests this statement was Agnaieff's idea; Agnaieff says the statement was initiated by Nakitsas in Ottawa at the request of Rémi Trudel; Nakitsas denies any responsibility.
10. Raymond Guardia interview, February 2, 1994.
11. McLaughlin, *A Woman's Place*, p. 100.
12. *Le Soleil,* December 7, 1989.
13. *Le Devoir,* editorial, December 7, 1989.
14. Knight says much of the money earmarked for Quebec TV ads was in fact shifted to more promising areas during the campaign. He estimates that campaign spending in Quebec amounted to between 10 and 15 per cent of the cross-Canada NDP total. Quebec provided 18 per cent of the party's total vote.
15. Philip Resnick, "Dividing in Two: A Test for Reason and Emotion," in Daniel Drache, ed., *Negotiating with a Sovereign Quebec* (Toronto: Lorimer, 1992), p. 84.
16. *La Presse,* editorial, November 28, 1991.
17. Alain Tassé interview, February 4, 1994.
18. Brian Topp interview, December 16, 1993.
19. Brian Topp interview, February 8, 1994.
20. Brian Topp interview, December 16, 1993.
21. John Richards interview, February 11, 1994.
22. Michel Agnaieff interview, February 4, 1994.
23. Maude Barlow and Bruce Campbell, *Take Back the Nation* (Toronto: Key Porter Books, 1991), p. 217.
24. John Richards, "The NDP in the Constitutional Drama," in Douglas Brown and Robert Young, eds., *Canada: The State of the Federation 1992* (Kingston: Institute of Intergovernmental Relations, Queen's University, 1992), p. 160. Audrey McLaughlin's book *A Woman's Place* avoids the issue of Quebec nationalism. She proposes to resolve the division of powers by asking questions like, "How much must the federal government be able to do to ensure the kind of country we want?" (p. 162).
25. Reg Whitaker, "The Quebec Question," in Simon Rosenblum and Peter Findlay, eds., *Debating Canada's Future: Views from the Left* (Toronto: Lorimer, 1991), p. 250.
26. Ian McLeod, memo to Audrey McLaughlin and Les Campbell, January 6, 1991.
27. Author's notes, December 16, 1991.
28. Barlow and Campbell, *Take Back the Nation*, p. 183.
29. *The Globe and Mail* August 31, 1992.
30. Les Campbell interview, April 6, 1994.
31. Gerald Caplan conversation, March 22, 1994.
32. Daniel Drache interview, January 25, 1994.
33. Michael Balagus interview, January 11, 1994.
34. David Perry interview, February 15, 1994.
35. Chris Axworthy interview, February 26, 1994.
36. McLaughlin, *A Woman's Place,* p. 167.
37. Michael Mandel, "Sovereignty and the New Constitutionalism," in Drache, ed., *Negotiating with a Sovereign Quebec,* p. 228.
38. McLaughlin, *A Woman's Place,* p. 171.

39. Lorne Nystrom interview, February 2, 1994.
40. Gerry Scott interview, February 15, 1994.
41. Audrey McLaughlin interview, March 17, 1994.
42. Philip Resnick, "Negotiating with Québec: A New Division of Powers or Secession?" in Drache, ed., *Negotiating with a Sovereign Quebec*, p. 89.
43. Audrey McLaughlin interview, March 17, 1994.

Chapter 6

1. Quoted in Whitehorn, *Canadian Socialism,* p. 234.
2. James Laxer interview, January 25, 1994.
3. Jon Pammett, "Tracking the Vote," Table 8, in Alan Frizzell, Jon Pammett, and Anthony Westell, eds., *The Canadian General Election 1993* (Ottawa: Carleton University Press, 1994).
4. Henry Milner and Arthur Milner, "Social Democracy versus Democratic Socialism: The Question of Public Ownership," in Rosenblum and Findlay, eds., *Debating Canada's Future*, pp. 11–12.
5. Ken Delaney, "Facing the Future and Facing Up to It," United Steelworkers, Toronto, unpublished, 1993 (photocopy).
6. Daniel Drache interview, January 25, 1994.
7. Doug Coupar interview, January 14, 1994.
8. Allan Blakeney, "The Social Democratic Challenge: To Manage both Production and Distribution," in John Richards, Robert Cairns, and Larry Pratt, eds., *Social Democracy Without Illusions* (Toronto: McClelland & Stewart, 1991), p. 54.
9. Allan Blakeney, remarks to a conference of private-sector unions, Toronto, May 6, 1994.
10. Allan Blakeney, in Richards, Cairns and Pratt, p. 50.
11. Audrey McLaughlin interview, *The Sudbury Star,* June 27, 1993.
12. Tommy Douglas interview, May 14, 1985.
13. Leo Panitch and Donald Swartz, "The Case for Socialist Democracy," in Rosenblum and Findlay, eds., *Debating Canada's Future,* p. 33.
14. Sam Gindin and David Robertson, *Democracy and Productive Capacity* (Ottawa: Canadian Centre for Policy Alternatives, 1991).
15. James Laxer, *Rethinking the Economy* (Toronto: NC Press, 1984), p. 2.
16. James Laxer interview, January 25, 1994.
17. Bob White, "Lost Opportunity: New Democrats let labour down," *Our Times,* January 1989.
18. Duncan Cameron, letter to Ed Broadbent, January 26, 1988 (photocopy).
19. John McCallum, "Economics and the New Democratic Party: Confessions of a One-Time NDPer," in Richards, Cairns and Pratt, eds., *Social Democracy Without Illusions,* p. 198.
20. Daniel Drache interview, January 25, 1994.
21. Henry Milner, "What Canadian Social Democrats Need to Know About Sweden, and Why," in Richards et al., eds., *Social Democracy Without Illusions,* p. 58.
22. Michael Balagus interview, January 12, 1994.
23. Dave Mackenzie interview, March 4, 1994.
24. Dave Mackenzie interview, March 4, 1994.
25. Judy Darcy, interview, April 25, 1994.
26. For example, *Benefits Canada* reported that at the end of 1993, the top 100 government and corporate pension plans in Canada held more than $260 billion in assets.
27. Michel Agnaieff interview, February 4, 1994.
28. *Canadian Dimension,* editorial, January–February 1994, p. 3.

29. David Mackenzie and André Foucault, "Rethinking Our Mission in Ontario," unpublished, November 1, 1993 (photocopy).
30. Joy Langan interview, February 9, 1994.
31. It should be noted that the establishment of worker control in industry would not kill the profit motive. Firms would continue to maximize profits and to experience friction with others in the community over tax rates (and thus support for social programs), environmental programs, and so on.

Chapter 7

1. *The Globe and Mail,* June 17, 1993.
2. Garry Aldridge, quoted in the Saskatoon *Star–Phoenix,* October 19, 1993.
3. Sandra Mitchell interview, February 7, 1993.
4. Jim Ryan interview, January 26, 1994.
5. Sandra Mitchell interview, February 7, 1994.
6. Carol Phillips memo to Michael Balagus, March 9, 1993.
7. Draft campaign strategy presented to full SEPC, April 17, 1993.
8. *The Globe and Mail,* June 17, 1993.
9. *The Toronto Star,* June 29, 1993.
10. Thunder Bay *Chronicle-Journal,* June 22, 1993.
11. Peter Boisseau, CP news wire, June 18, 1993.
12. Stewart MacLeod, St John's *Evening Telegram,* June 21, 1993.
13. Audrey McLaughlin letter to the NDP, n.d., draft, copy. It was mailed to candidates on July 30, two weeks after McLaughlin's offer to resign.
14. *Winnipeg Free Press,* editorial, August 13, 1993.
15. *The Globe and Mail,* August 14, 1993.
16. Michael Lewis interview, January 24, 1994.
17. Audrey McLaughlin, "Opening Statement," dated September 1993 (photocopy).
18. Jim Ryan interview, January 26, 1994.
19. Dave Mackenzie interview, March 4, 1994.
20. Daniel Drache interview, January 25, 1994.
21. NDP Research memo to NDP caucus, February 16, 1993, based on Elections Canada public reports.
22. "English Debate Opening Statement by Audrey McLaughlin," October 4, 1993.
23. John Brewin interview, February 2, 1994.
24. Dawn Black interview, February 10, 1994.
25. David Perry interview, February 15, 1994.
26. Chris Axworthy interview, March 1, 1994.
27. Ian Waddell conversation, March 31, 1994.
28. John Brewin interview, February 2, 1994.
29. Doug Coupar interview, January 11, 1994.
30. Federal NDP fundraising letter, August 23, 1994.
31. Tony Clarke interview, January 29, 1994.

Chapter 8

1. Peter Bleyer interview, January 28, 1994.
2. *The Globe and Mail,* September 22, 1989.
3. This axis later appointed 10 additional members from the short-lived New Party Clubs to represent "liberally minded individuals."
4. Alan Whitehorn, "Some Preliminary Reflections on the Labour Movement and the New Democratic Party," December 1, 1993 version (photocopy), p. 13.
5. Robert White, "Lost Opportunity: New Democrats Let Labour Down," *Our Times,* January 1989.

6. Bob White, "From Defeat to Renewal: The NDP Tomorrow," *This Magazine,* May–June 1989.
7. White, "From Defeat to Renewal: The NDP Tomorrow."
8. Geoff Bickerton, "White must confront weakness of CLC," *Canadian Dimension,* March 1992.
9. Stuart Crombie, "Rule Breaker, Movement Maker: Bob White and the CLC," *Our Times,* May 1992.
10. See Vickers, et al., *Politics As If Women Mattered,* p. 58; Gagnon and Tanguay, eds., *Canadian Parties in Transition;* John Meisel, "The Decline of Party in Canada," in Hugh Thorburn, ed., *Party Politics in Canada,* 5th edition (Scarborough: Prentice-Hall, 1985); and William Carroll, ed., *Organizing Dissent* (Toronto: Garamond Press, 1992).
11. Harold Clarke and Allan Kornberg, "Evaluations and Evolution: Public Attitudes toward Canada's Federal Political Parties, 1965–1991," *Canadian Journal of Political Science,* June 1993.
12. Rick Salutin, from "Waiting for Democracy," in Brooks, ed., *Canadian Democracy,* p. 205.
13. Mona-Josée Gagnon, "Trade Unions in Quebec: New Stakes," in Leys and Mendell, eds., *Culture and Social Change* (Montreal: Black Rose, 1992), p. 63.
14. Robert White, "Unions and coalitions: broadening the base," *Action Canada Dossier* #37, May–June 1992.
15. See Peter Bleyer, "Coalitions of Social Action Movements as Agencies for Social Change: The Action Canada Network," in Carroll, ed., *Organizing Dissent.*
16. Judy Darcy interview, April 25, 1994.
17. Louis Favreau, "The 'Backyard Revolution' in Quebec: People and Community in a Liberal Democracy," in Leys and Mendell, eds., *Culture and Social Change.*
18. Vickers et al., *Politics As If Women Mattered,* p. 291.
19. Judy Rebick interview, April 8, 1994.
20. Tony Clarke interview, January 31, 1994.
21. Chris Axworthy interview, March 1, 1994.
22. Chris Axworthy interview, March 1, 1994.
23. John Brewin interview, February 2, 1994.
24. Judy Rebick interview, April 8, 1994.
25. Joy Langan interview, February 9, 1994.
26. Michael Balagus interview, January 20, 1994.
27. Peter Bleyer interview, January 28, 1994.
28. Judy Rebick interview, April 8, 1994.
29. Audrey McLaughlin interview, March 17, 1994.
30. Geraldine McGuire, quoted in the Vancouver *Sun,* November 19, 1994.
31. Buzz Hargrove, letter to Jack Grant, member of NDP Ontario provincial council, February 23, 1994 (photocopy).
32. Buzz Hargrove interview, March 3, 1994.
33. David Mackenzie and André Foucault, "Rethinking our mission in Ontario," November 1, 1993 draft (photocopy).
34. *Winnipeg Free Press,* October 28 and November 18, 1993.
35. John Richards, "Playing Two Games at Once," in Richards, Cairns and Pratt, eds., *Social Democracy Without Illusions,* p. 116.
36. U.K. Labour Party, "Trade Unions and the Labour Party," 1993[?].
37. Judy Darcy interview, April 25, 1994.
38. Canada's New Democrats, "New Democrat Renewal Workbook," March 24, 1994.
39. Buzz Hargrove, "Desperately Seeking the NDP," *Our Times,* March 1993.

Chapter 9

1. Canada's New Democrats, "New Democrat Renewal Workbook," March 24, 1994.
2. Canada's New Democrats, "New Democrat Renewal Workbook," March 24, 1994.
3. Delia Carley, "Party leaders bending democratic principle," *The Ottawa Citizen,* May 9, 1994.
4. Tony Pennikett, remarks to NDP Federal Council, January 29, 1994.
5. John Sewell interview, February 21, 1994.
6. Joy Langan interview, February 9, 1994.
7. Duncan Cameron interview January 19, 1994.
8. James Laxer interview, January 25, 1994.
9. John Sewell interview, February 21, 1994.
10. Peter Julian interview, February 4, 1994.
11. Audrey McLaughlin, notes for remarks to the Canadian Labour Congress, May 18, 1994, 5-page final draft.
12. "Socialism 2000," United Workers' Party of Israel (Mapam), June 1993.
13. Audrey McLaughlin interview, March 17, 1994.
14. Tony Clarke interview, January 31, 1994.
15. Ed Broadbent, "Introduction," in Rosenblum and Findlay, eds., *Debating Canada's Future.*
16. Doug Coupar conversation, June 4, 1994.
17. Tony Pennikett, remarks to NDP Federal Council, January 29, 1994.
18. James Laxer interview, January 25, 1994.
19. David Mackenzie and André Foucault, "Rethinking our mission in Ontario," November 1 1993 draft, unpublished.
20. Chris Axworthy interview, March 1, 1994.
21. Gerry Scott, "We Know What Happened — Now Let's Talk About Why," February 1994, unpublished.
22. Gerry Scott interview, May 15, 1994.
23. Audrey McLaughlin interview, March 17, 1994.
24. Salem Bland, speech at Alhambra Hall, Toronto, October 3, 1933, from notes at the United Church Archives, Toronto.

Bibliography

Barlow, Maude, and Bruce Campbell. *Take Back the Nation*. Toronto: Key Porter Books, 1991.

Brooks, Stephen. *Canadian Democracy: An Introduction*. Toronto: McClelland & Stewart, 1993.

Canada's New Democrats. *Strategy for a Full-Employment Economy*. Ottawa, 1993.

Carroll, William C., ed. *Organizing Dissent: Contemporary Social Movements in Theory and Practice*. Toronto: Garamond Press, 1992.

Cohen, Andrew. *A Deal Undone: The Making and Breaking of the Meech Lake Accord*. Vancouver: Douglas & McIntyre, 1990.

Drache, Daniel, ed. *Getting on Track: Social Democratic Strategies for Ontario*. Montreal & Kingston: McGill-Queen's University Press, 1992.

Drache, Daniel, and Roberto Perin, eds. *Negotiating with a Sovereign Quebec*. Toronto: James Lorimer and Company, 1992.

Gagnon, Alain G., and A. Brian Tanguay, eds. *Canadian Parties in Transition*. Scarborough: Nelson Canada, 1991.

Gindin, Sam, and David Robertson. *Democracy and Productive Capacity*. Ottawa: Canadian Centre for Policy Alternatives, 1991.

Hall, Stuart, and Martin Jacques, eds. *New Times*. New York: Verso, 1990.

Harrington, Michael. *The Next Left*. New York: Henry Holt, 1987.

Heaps, Leo, ed. *Our Canada: The Story of the New Democratic Party Yesterday, Today and Tomorrow*. Toronto: James Lorimer and Company, 1991.

Laxer, James. *Inventing Europe: The Rise of a New World Power*. Toronto: Lester Publishing, 1991.

Laxer, James. *Re-Thinking the Economy*. Toronto: NC Press, 1984.

Leys, Colin, and Marguerite Mendell. *Culture and Social Change*. Montreal: Black Rose Books, 1992.

McDonald, Lynn. *The Party That Changed Canada*. Toronto: Macmillan of Canada, 1987.

McLaughlin, Audrey, with Rick Archbold. *A Woman's Place: My Life and Politics*. Toronto: MacFarlane Walter & Ross, 1992.

Morton, Desmond. *The New Democrats 1961–1986*. Toronto: Copp Clark Pitman, 1986.

Ontario Ministry of Industry. *An Industrial Policy Framework for Ontario*. Toronto, July 1992.

Osborne, David, and Ted Gaebler. *Reinventing Government*. New York: Penguin Books USA, 1993.

Richards, John, Robert Cairns, and Larry Pratt, eds. *Social Democracy Without Illusions: Renewal of the Canadian Left*. Toronto: McClelland & Stewart, 1991.

Richards, John, and Don Kerr, eds. *Canada, What's Left? A New Social Contract Pro and Con*. Edmonton: NeWest Press, 1986.

Roberts, Wayne, and George Ehring. *Giving Away a Miracle*. Oakville, Ont.: Mosaic Press, 1993.

Rosenblum, Simon, and Peter Findlay, eds. *Debating Canada's Future: Views from the Left*. Toronto: James Lorimer and Company, 1991.

Vickers, Jill, Pauline Rankin, and Christine Appelle. *Politics As If Women Mattered: A Political Analysis of the National Action Committee on the Status of Women*. Toronto: University of Toronto Press, 1993.

Wearing, Joseph. *Strained Relations — Canadian Voters and Parties*. Toronto: McClelland & Stewart, 1988.

Whitehorn, Alan. *Canadian Socialism: Essays on the CCF-NDP*. Toronto: Oxford University Press, 1992.

Index

1984 federal election campaign, 21, 22
1987 federal convention, 68-9
1988 federal election campaign, 24, 27, 69-70
1989 leadership campaign, vi, 12, 27-32, 134, 142
1990 federal by-election, Montreal, 72
1991 summer convention Halifax, 14, 47
1993 federal election campaign, vi, 9, 66, 100-15; NDP objective in, 100; promotional video, 107; town hall forum, 106-7

aboriginal issues, vii, 10, 31, 41, 66, 72, 73, 75, 77, 79, 84, 87, 111
abortion, 36, 58
Action Canada Network, 7, 59-60, 81, 114, 119, 120, 121-2; anti-GST campaign, 59
affirmative action, 34, 35, 36, 47, 105, 111
Agnaieff, Michel, 49, 68-9, 72, 151n. 9
Alberta NDP, 22, 103
Anguish, Doug, 20
Axworthy, Chris, 53, 56, 79, 112-13, 122, 143

Balagus, Michael, 37, 40, 55, 62, 78-9, 94-5, 100-1, 102, 107; background of, 44; campaign strategy, 33, 102, 105; dealings with MPs, 55; on Gulf War, 58; McLaughlin's support of, 63, 108; on NAFTA and GST campaigns, 94; resignation, 107; staff relations, 45-6
Barlow, Maude, 72, 76, 80
Barrett, Dave, 28, 43, 54, 56, 60, 112; leadership campaign, 29-30, 142; on Quebec, 29
bilingualism, 66, 143
Black, Dawn, 47, 53, 59, 111, 123, 131, 133
Blakeney, Allan, viii, 12, 29, 44; on deficits, 88; opposition to Broadbent, 20
Bland, Dr. Salem, 1, 146
Bleyer, Peter, 10
Bloc Québécois, vii, 1
Bourassa, Robert, 77
Brewin, John, 13, 28, 38, 50, 56, 58, 61, 111, 113, 123
British Columbia NDP, 14, 15, 93, 110, 113, 124, 136. See also Harcourt, Mike.
Broadbent, Edward (Ed), 3, 6, 16, 18, 19-20, 21, 32, 51, 54, 55, 67-70, 73, 98, 118, 141; on language rights, 70; leadership of, 22-8
Brown, Rosemary, 20, 28

Cameron, Duncan, 92, 136
Campbell, Les, 34, 44-6, 49, 50, 55-6, 72, 76, 102, 137; background, 44; campaign strategy, 33; and Lorne Nystrom, 55-6; resignation, 62
Campbell, Kim, 43, 59, 104
Canada 2000, 13
Canadian Auto Workers (CAW), 8, 63, 91-2, 97-8, 117, 127
Canadian Labour Congress (CLC), 26, 53, 87, 91-2, 95, 117, 119, 124, 127, 129, 130, 140
Canadian Union of Public Employees (CUPE), 96-7, 120, 127, 129
capitalism, 4, 5, 6, 8, 89, 129
Caplan, Gerald, 20, 21, 75, 78
CCF (Co-operative Commonwealth Federation), 2, 7, 10, 19, 86, 88, 117
centralism, 67, 72
Charlottetown Accord, vii, 77, 79, 123
Charter of Rights, 69, 75
child care, 36
Chrétien, Jean, 28, 42, 101, 108, 110, 134, 138
Clark, Joe, 74, 75
Clarke, Tony, 7-8, 60, 114, 122, 141
Co-operative Commonwealth Federation. See CCF.
Conference on Socialism in Canada, 38
constituent assembly, 73, 75
Constitution, Canadian, 12, 20, 47, 51, 55, 59, 73; "Canada round" of negotiations, 72, 76, 77, 80. See also constitutional referendum, Yes committee.
constitutional referendum (1994), 59, 62, 66, 78
convention process, 13
corporate agenda, 4, 6, 31, 65, 87, 97
Council of Canadians, 114, 119
Coupar, Doug, 11, 87, 113, 142

Davis, Julie, 33, 102, 104, 106, 107, 128
de Jong, Simon, 30
Dewar, Marion, 14, 27, 35, 36, 37, 39, 47, 56, 112
Dobbin, Murray, 59
Docquier, Gerard, 24
Doer, Gary, 44, 47
Douglas, Tommy, 6, 17, 25, 32, 51, 147n. I.2; on capitalism, 89; influ-

ence on NDP, 18; as leader, 19; on Quebec, 80

Drache, Daniel, 10, 78, 83-4, 87, 110-11

Edmonston, Phil, 49, 54, 64, 65, 71, 73

environment, 7, 22, 23, 38, 59, 76, 87, 88, 123, 124, 142

Europe, 75, 80, 90, 91, 97

Federal Council, 14, 51, 70, 77, 131, 133

federal deficit, 22, 26, 86, 92, 96

feminism, 24, 36-8, 40, 41, 43, 124, 142

free trade, 4, 23, 27, 59, 61, 78, 91, 95, 117

Free Trade Agreement (FTA), 4, 7, 69, 95, 119

Fulton, Jim, 52, 65

Gardiner, Brian, 61

gay and lesbian issues, 31, 52, 120, 143

Gerard, Leo, 30

Goods and Services Tax (GST), 59, 60, 93, 94, 95, 119, 123

Gotthilf, David, 21, 46, 137

government regulation, 8

Green, Fraser, v, 101, 102, 104, 106, 107

Gulf War, 57

Gwynn, Richard, 26

Harcourt, Mike, 12, 15, 63, 75, 88, 123

Hargrove, Buzz, 106, 127, 130

Harney, Jean-Paul, 67, 68, 69, 70

Health care, 4, 22, 76, 88, 112

Heap, Dan, 52

homelessness, 5, 6

Jobs Plan, 14, 59, 60, 85, 86, 87, 95-6, 97, 103, 110-11

Karpoff, Jim, 52

Knight, Bill, 12, 25, 44, 70, 78, 102, 151n. 14; resignation, 25

Knowles, Stanley, 18, 20, 50, 117

labour, 3, 7, 8, 25, 29, 69, 79, 87, 90, 95, 100, 106, 117, 118, 124, 130, 146, 153n. 31; and coalitions, 119; financial support of NDP, 128; in Quebec, 67, 69, 70, 71, 80; and Rae government, 113, 127; and worker-management alliances, 26, 96-8

Labour Party (U.K.), 129

Langan, Joy, 28, 31, 52, 54, 59, 98, 124, 136, 142

Langdon, Steven, 54, 62-4, 95, 108, 115

Laxer, James, 4, 11, 26, 91, 108, 115

League for Social Reconstruction, 10

Lewis, David, vi, 18, 19, 20, 51, 117, 147n. I.2

Lewis, Michael, 39, 108, 110, 113

Lewis, Stephen, 19, 27, 102

Liberal Party, v, vii, 3, 4, 6, 12, 21, 23, 25, 61, 66, 78, 79, 85, 87, 97, 101, 114, 116, 124, 127, 137, 147n. I.4; "Red Book," 11, 96, 110, 138

Mackenzie, David (Dave), 95, 96, 110, 128

Macphail, Agnes, 18

Manitoba NDP, 14, 137

Manning, Preston, 42, 43, 78, 101, 114, 134

market economy, viii, 6, 8, 89, 99, 140

Marxism, 86, 89, 90

McCurdy, Howard, 10, 64, 76, 95, 142

McDermott, Dennis, 26

McDonough, Alexa, 27, 28, 33, 39, 131

McKee, Brian, 13

McLaughlin, Audrey, vi, vii, viii, 3, 13, 16, 17-18, 33-47, 49-50, 53-8, 60-4, 82-4, 85, 88, 93-6, 98, 100-111, 113, 115, 118, 121, 122, 123-4, 126, 131-3, 134-5, 137, 140-42, 145-6; background, 39, 40; campaign promises, 31, 38, 118; and the Constitution, 47, 72, 73, 75, 76; discipline of MPs, 54; and feminism, 34, 36, 40, 41-2; Gulf War speeches, 58; lack of political experience of, vi, 28, 32, 35, 39, 51; leadership campaign, 28, 29-30, 34, 142; leadership style, 54, 134; and the media, 17, 28, 33, 40, 42-3, 62, 104; opposition to, 54, 56; public perception of, 18, 20, 102, 104, 109; and Quebec, 71, 80, 82-3, 151n. 24; resignation, viii, 132

McLelland, Richard, 107

media, vi, 22, 38, 42-3, 51, 56, 57, 60, 62, 64, 89, 104; in Quebec, 68, 69, 71, 129

Meech Lake Accord, 22, 27, 67, 70

Members of Parliament: pensions, 49-51; working conditions, 52;

Mercredi, Ovide, 79

Mexico, 5, 94

Mitchell, Sandra, 57, 62, 64, 75, 101, 102

Morton, Desmond, 11, 93

Mulroney, Brian, 21, 23, 24, 62, 72, 76, 77-8, 91, 102

multiculturalism, 66

NAFTA (North American Free Trade Agreement), 5, 7, 60, 61, 93, 94, 101, 103, 110, 138

Nakitsas, George, 25, 27, 67, 68, 69, 70, 102, 151n. 9

National Action Committee on the Status of Women (NAC), 12, 111, 120, 121, 123-4

NATO, 22, 24

Natural Law Party, vi
New Democratic Party (NDP), affiliation with unions, 117; and dissent, 11-13; economic policy, 26, 85-99; formation of, 2, 66, 117; funding of, 14-15, 104, 111, 117, 128, 135; and grass roots, 11-12, 22, 116; and intellectuals, 10-11, 87; as permanent party of opposition, 3; power structure of, 51, 137-8; public support for, v, vi, vii, 63, 86, 109, 115, 147n. I.4; relationship to provincial parties, 14-16, 92-3, 113; renewal process, vii, 1-16, 31, 131, 133-46; and special interest groups, 111-12, 116, 122-7, 145; use of polls by, 9, 21, 109, 114-15; women in, vi, 36-7, 38, 47
New Social Movement Theory, 119, 126, 128
Notley, Grant, 12
Nystrom, Lorne, 20, 27, 34, 55, 64, 65, 73-5, 81, 131

Oliver, Michael, 10
"one-third world," 5
Ontario Federation of Labour, 127, 128
Ontario NDP, 8, 93, 113, 127

Parizeau, Jacques, 82
Parti Québécois, 67, 68, 69
pay equity, 36, 127
pension plans for MPs, 49-51
Policy and Issues Group, 95
Proctor, Dick, 38, 46, 101
Progressive Conservative party, v, vi, vii, 3, 4, 12, 39, 54, 61, 66, 74, 80, 101, 102, 124, 127

Quebec, vii, 10, 22, 24, 27, 29, 66-84, 97, 151n. 14/ 151n. 24
Quebec NDP, 22, 68, 70, 71

Rae, Bob, 3, 15, 47, 63, 64, 75, 76, 77, 80, 103, 104, 104, 106, 115, 117; as potential federal leader, 29;
Reagan, Ronald, 21
Rebick, Judy, 36, 40, 41, 121, 123-4, 126
Reform Party, vii, 1, 7, 61, 66, 101, 102, 110, 112, 114, 123, 136, 143, 144
Richards, John, 11, 12, 72, 73
Riche, Nancy, 76, 104, 118, 132
Riis, Nelson, 7, 15, 27, 28, 32, 39, 40, 58, 64, 132, 143
Robinson, Svend, 52, 64, 65
Rodriguez, John, 52, 64, 112
Romanow, Roy, 12, 15, 53, 63, 75, 88, 104, 107
Ryan, Jim, 109, 110

Saskatchewan NDP, 14, 88, 93, 113, 137
Schreyer, Ed, 28

Scott, Frank, 67
Scott, Gerry, 8, 82, 143-4
Senate, 74
Sewell, John, 135, 139
Sihota, Moe, 77
social action groups, vi, 2, 12, 31, 37, 80, 87, 116, 119, 120, 122, 125, 126, 127, 129, 139, 146
social charter, 73, 75-6, 79, 80
social contract, 90, 93, 104, 106
social democracy, vi, vii, viii, 3, 4, 8, 25, 26, 86-7, 89, 142; versus socialism, 89-90, 141
social programs, vii, 4, 5, 31, 86, 90, 92, 121, 117, 121, 153n. 31
Standing, Guy, 5
Steelworkers, 8, 29, 39, 97-8, 127, 128
Strategic and Election Planning Committee (SEPC), 95, 101, 102, 103-4, 105, 106, 107, 108
Sweden, 10, 69, 90, 95-6

Thobani, Sunera, 123
tobacco tax, 52
Topp, Brian, 71, 72
Trudeau, Pierre, 21, 39, 44
Trudel, Rémi, 68
Turner, John, 21, 23

"Us and Them" approach, 6, 8, 19, 21, 30, 36, 62, 85, 86, 87, 93, 97, 99, 104, 108; in Ontario NDP, 93; reasons for, 86-7

VIA rail, 31, 59
Vickers, Jill, 18, 37, 39

Waffle movement, 11
War Measures Act (1972), 51, 58
Welfare state, 79, 91
Western Canada, viii, 14, 20, 29, 54, 72, 78, 101, 123, 138, 143
White, Robert (Bob), 29, 30, 64, 115, 116-17, 118-19, 120, 125, 128, 129; criticism of Broadbent, 24-5; as potential NDP leader, 27
Whitehorn, Alan, 13, 27, 47
Women, vi, vii, 35-7, 38, 39, 42-3, 46, 54, 72, 121
Woodsworth, James (J.S.), 2, 17
Worker ownership, 25, 90, 98, 153n. 31

Yes committee, vii, 67, 77-8, 112
York, Geoffrey, 43, 104
Youth, vii, 3, 9-10, 14, 35, 38, 75, 138-9